HOW TO START A GHOST
KITCHEN DELIVERY SERVICE

By Hitachi Choparazzi

Acknowledgements

To the Creator of the universe! My sons Kolany Jr., Pierre Kydale, and Kylan. My family Mama Lisa, all of my sisters and brothers, especially Ginger. I love y'all. I know you and the world will appreciate my literary works. May God bless all my deceased Luvıs souls and my Dayıs. I miss and love y'all, too.

ATTN:

This *How to Start a Ghost Kitchen Delivery Service* book is written from the author Hitachi Choparazzi's perspective as an analysis and thru his ghost kitchen experience.

All public data, trademarks, etc., belong to their respective owners, entities, or shareholders respectively. Any and all data that is used in this book is to give readers recent factual basis of proven information, systems, and analytics.

This book is not for you to have guaranteed instant success for your ghost kitchen delivery start-up business. Nor by reading this book guarantee you instant riches to automatically make you a small fortune.

The author Hitachi Choparazzi is not a financial advisor, broker, nor consultant. This book is not to advise you financially. This book is merely to educate you how to start your own ghost kitchen delivery service from author's perspective and personal experience with a ghost kitchen.

Contents

Prologue

I want to start off by thanking all of you for taking the time to read this book, whether traditional, via ebook, or Audible. It shows that you are eager to learn, dedicated, serious or just simply curious and out weighing your options. All is welcome!

However, there is no need to be one foot out and one foot in. After you read this book, you should be both feet all in, or both feet all out. Capitalize on the growing demand.

I first want to take the time out to clarify before going any further into the how-to book, that this book is not to be confused for how to build your own ghost kitchen facility. That could be upwards well into six to seven figures. This book is to show how to start a ghost kitchen and delivery service in one of the many ghost kitchen facilities popping up all over the U.S. nation and globally. Some of these ghost kitchen hubs or facilities are private and public, too.

I will show how to rent or lease from these trendy kitchen facilities to start your own virtual kitchen space and menu board to multiple delivery service platforms accordingly and featured.

This is why I took the time out to sit down, and manually, really handwrite this *How to Start a Ghost Kitchen* book, in chronological order to simplify, provide resources, and information, to make your first-step kitchen and delivery service journey and educated knowledgeable transition to your own actual hands-on experience. It shouldn't be too complex.

Now let's get started, shall we. Please enjoy and use each chapter title as a directory guide to go back, and reread as needed. May God bless all of restaurateurs in your ghost kitchen start-ups, and the food service your virtual menu board provides to the public. Remember food is essential: we need it to sustain life, and it's also social, brings family and friends or colleagues to sit down together at the table and eat!

- Chapter 1 -

"What Is a Ghost Kitchen?"

Food is fun, and one of the greatest experiences as humans. As a foodie, I can tell you this thru experience. Food is community, and should be a variety best in taste. Food is family. Food is social. Food is culture. The power food has to bring community, family, and friends together.

Three years ago I, Hitachi Choparazzi, wrote *How to Start-up a Food Truck Business*. That was in 2019. Which food truck movements was continuously popping up all across the U.S., threatening restaurant space with a competitive fraction of the price you'd find at restaurants. However, now with these new commercial kitchens on demand known now as ghost kitchens, again the restaurant space and owners are forced to adapt or opt out of business for closure.

We will discuss that further in this how to do a ghost kitchen delivery service book. All the pros and cons, through my personal experience in two ghost kitchens in the Phoenix and Tempe areas of Arizona. Therefore, whether foodie, restaurateurs, or just an investor, I will leave you with a bunch of knowledge, tips, and bonus thru experience to give you reality to make a formative decision in this new ghost kitchen space.

During 2020 pandemic the cause of COVID-19 lockdown had delivery services up, and a surge in profit margins, which helped delivery become the new norm, and delivery platforms mainstream, and most of all a fortune.

Let's say it's a weekend and you're hungry. Already off work and comfortable in your home with your family. Then you unlock your smartphone and open up one of the delivery apps to scroll through a virtual buffet roster of options. A listing catches your eyes. Pierre's Fish and Chips! You may never heard of the place? However, the food, clearly displayed in enticing mouthwatering photos, looks delicious. Next, you add a two-piece fried cod with fries ($12.95) to your cart and a dozen of mango habanero wings ($14.95), and hit order. Then a notification pops up: DELIVERY ETA 25-40 minutes.

Meanwhile, downtown in an industrial area by the airport in a signless storefront, your fish and chips and 12 mango habanero wings order pops onto a tablet screen with a loud ping to alert and notify staff. A cook working the line takes note and tosses a few filets and fries into the fryer along with a dozen mango habanero wings in another fryer. All while putting the finishing touches on a few other orders: a vegan fried patty and a roast beef and quinoa salad.

This is what is called a ghost kitchen, sometimes referred to as "virtual," "cloud," "shadow," or "dark" kitchens. Ghost kitchens offer restaurateurs multiple benefits, too, we will discuss as well.

A ghost kitchen is a restaurant that serves its food exclusively for consumption off-premises. Most ghost kitchens are delivery-only and solely accept orders online through first-party and third-party platforms. Some ghost kitchens, however, do offer take-out or drive-thru options, though these restaurants are the exception to the norm. By 2030, it's expected that ghost kitchens will make up 50% of the take-out and drive-thru dining sectors.

Ghost kitchens can operate as a stand-alone business for new restaurateurs to test their concepts. However, they can also act as brand extensions from notable restaurant businesses.

For example, ghost kitchen It's Just Wings actually shares a parent company with Chili's.

Now, this next ghost kitchen space was previously home to Michael Cimarusti's Cape Seafood and Provisions, a restaurant and market that closed in early 2019. However, since late 2020, the tenant has been Byte to Bite Industries, a market-leading virtual restaurant owner and operator with different locations.

Whereas, they are not restaurants in the traditional sense, Byte to Bite locations prepare food for the 30 delivery-only brands the company owns or licenses, including Fisher & Sons, Angel Wings, Burger Bitch, Morning After Breakfast, No Joke PB&J, and Nacho Lords.

Whether you order your fish and chips from Fisher & Sons or one of the company's two other seafood concepts, Sunset Beach Fish & Chips and The Codfather, the same two pieces of our famous ale-battered Pacific cod and crispy French fries served with tartar sauce that each brand offers will be cooked in the same kitchen by the same crew. And that crew will be tasked with preparing quinoa salad, mango habanero wings or whatever brand-specific orders appear on the tablet.

Across Los Angeles, these tech-enabled transactions occur each day with thousands of orders, hundreds of drivers, dozens of ghost kitchens hidden in strip malls or freeway-adjacent industrial areas.

Furthermore, in a remarkably short span, LA has become a national epicenter for this booming business, one that has attracted billions in industry investment and, fueled by a restaurant-crippling pandemic, has the potential to fundamentally reshape the way we dine and the market.

The ghost-kitchen economy, it would seem, is here to stay. The building houses commercial kitchens providing orders for delivery services and for take-out. Even before COVID-19 arrived, food delivery apps had begun reshaping the restaurant industry. A growing number of people were ordering food to eat at home, and a significant portion of those sales were facilitated through apps.

In 2018, the financial research firm UBS projected that the global food delivery market would grow 13.5% annually for the foreseeable future, compared with 3% growth in overall restaurant industry. And that was before the pandemic hit.

As demand for food delivery has skyrocketed, the definition of what constitutes a restaurant has become increasingly flexible. Renting space for a dining room? Wait staff? Table and chairs? Optional.

The only requirement is a kitchen. Focused solely on fulfilling online orders, these ghost-kitchen restaurants market their food directly to delivery app users, leaving some customers largely unaware that their restaurant does not physically exist as a separate brick-and-mortar facility.

One of the few experts chronicling the growth of this nascent industry is Matt Newberg, a tech industry veteran who in 2019 founded HNGRY, a media event platform that seeks to examine the impact of technology on our relationship with food.

According to Newberg, there is no singular type of ghost kitchen. Though there are several configurations that have become increasingly popular.

The simplest way are those that piggyback off a real-life restaurant, using existing kitchens to offer new cuisines or concepts available exclusively on delivery apps. A brick-and-mortar restaurant that specializes in French food, for example, might pull double duty as a delivery-only sandwich brand.

The idea of a ghost kitchen is really a paradox, because of course you can't scale kitchen space the way Amazon scales servers, but that's the way tech companies are approaching it.

One example is Virtual Restaurant Consulting, a Los Angeles-based start-up that partners with restaurateurs to launch profitable take-out and delivery-only restaurants in their existing kitchens in as little as 30 days. According to the company's website, orders for delivery and take-out are notified via phone at West & Mel food company, in Los Angeles. The building houses commercial kitchens cooking up participating restaurants' dishes.

According to promotional materials released in March of 2021, a restaurant can purchase, for a monthly license fee of $249.00 and an 18% cut of sales for the first six months, a license to operate Two Hens, a VRC-owned all-day breakfast brand, out of its kitchen, with the company providing menu training programs, social media and web pages, and streamlined access to third-party delivery platforms.

On top of the rising costs, labor shortages, stifling regulations, and brutal competition, independent restaurants are facing a growing shift toward off-premises dining, allowing restaurateurs to focus on cooking during the critical launch period of their new business while ghost kitchens manage everything else.

It's not just consulting companies looking to expand. LA investors with little to no experience in the restaurant business have poured millions into the construction of shared kitchen spaces, which offer fully equipped and permitted food prep areas that businesses can lease and staff in exchange for monthly rent and a percentage of sales.

One of the first and largest of these companies is City Storage Systems, an LA-based start-up co-founded by serial tech entrepreneur Diego Berdakin. According to business filings, the company focus involves repurposing distressed real estate assets, such as parking lots or abandoned commercial buildings, and turning them into facilities suited for new industries such as online retail or food delivery.

In 2015, Berdakin purchased a block-long, single-story warehouse in Pico-Union and spent the next two years outfitting the space with 27 kitchen units, each about 200 square feet. Situated across the street from a cemetery and scrawled with graffiti, the industrial warehouse didn't appear attractive as a traditional restaurant space but proved a perfect fit for one City Storage Systems subsidiary, Cloud Kitchens.

Soon Cloud Kitchens had filled its stalls with a dozen or so kitchens, with many licensing several of Cloud Kitchens' in-house brands for an additional fee. This meant the warehouse could be home to as many as 100 virtual listings, including Skinny Bitch Pizza, the Steve Aoki branded Pizzaoki, and Made in Brooklyn NY Pizza.

Two years after Cloud Kitchens' launch, Travis Kalanick, co-founder and former chief executive of Uber, bought a controlling interest in the company for $150 million, becoming its chief executive in early 2019. By the end of the year, the company had raised $400 million from Saudi Arabia's Sovereign Wealth Fund, an equity investment that valued Cloud Kitchens at about $5 billion, according to the *Wall Street Journal*.

The upside of a Cloud Kitchens' space is that your time to market is short and the upfront cost is low, said Noah Holton-Raphael, one of the co-owners of Ggiata, a Jersey-inspired Italian deli and Cloud Kitchens tenant who signed a month-to-month lease at Cloud Kitchens after shelving plans to launch Ggiata as a food truck. They estimate it took about $20,000 to open the deli as a delivery and take-out concept, which included hiring and training their own kitchen staff.

Rows of shipping containers were used to create the small kitchens inside the Grand Food Depot, a Cloud Kitchens facility near USC.

Having heavily invested in branding and the digital marketing, Ggiata was able to develop a sizable fan base for its sandwiches despite many customers being unaware that the restaurant was located inside a Cloud Kitchens commissary.

However, despite growing sales, the rest of the owners said they chafed at certain aspects of the Cloud Kitchens arrangement, including requirements that tenants use the company's proprietary software and have all orders handled by Cloud Kitchens staffers once they leave the kitchen.

As a business owner, it can be frustrating when you cannot control the entire experience.

Since launching in Pico-Union, Cloud Kitchens has expanded rapidly, opening ghost kitchen commissaries in Koreatown, Long Beach, Anaheim, and downtown. The company also has opened or acquired dozens of locations in cities across the country: Philadelphia, Oakland, Chicago, Houston, Atlanta, San Diego, Orlando, Columbus, Ohio, with most strategically located next to college campuses or urban centers.

Competing facilities have cropped up as well. There is Kitchen United in Pasadena, located in a former Le Cordon Bleu cooking school and home to 20 kitchen spaces, filled by tenants such as El Tepeyac Café, the Halal Guys, and Mama Musubi.

Another is Colony, a West LA shared kitchen facility founded by two German real estate investors that houses 37 brands including Trejo's Tacos, Sen Gumi, and Oi Asian Fusion.

Unlike Cloud Kitchens facilities, which allow customers to pick up orders but are mainly geared towards delivery drivers, Kitchen United and Colony have sought to cultivate the ambiance of a food court, installing outdoor seating, on-site ordering kiosks or drive-thru pick-up windows.

During COVID-19, however, the compact footprints that make commissary facilities appealing for developers have also made them a liability.

Whereas, during peak order times, drivers at some locations have reported issues with overcrowding at pick-up counters. At a Cloud Kitchens facility near USC, drivers are instructed to wait in their cars after checking in, while cramped kitchens areas offer hazardously little room for workers to socially distance.

Even as demand for food delivery has increased dramatically since the closure of indoor dining, sales grew 174% year-over-year as of mid-August 2021. According to a top analysis firm, companies such as Cloud Kitchens are facing new competition from vacant spaces that once housed traditional restaurants, another consequence of the pandemic.

That's the case with former Good Geek Grill restaurant space in Hollywood, now a commissary kitchen operated by GrubHub and the company behind Buca di Beppo in partnership with LA celebrity chef Eric Greenspan, an early adopter in the food delivery industry and former Cloud Kitchens partner.

The group recently launched Tyga Bites, a celebrity-owned virtual dining concept with Tyga's own chicken nuggets, different sauce and more, backed by the rapper Tyga.

Customer orders inside the kitchen of Taco Pete at the Grand Food Depot. Taco Pete, which has been in business for over 30 years in Compton, is expanding their reach by renting a space inside one of many ghost-kitchen facilities throughout LA area.

Or consider Spring, a lauded French fine dining spot in downtown LA that closed in 2018. What used to be a stunning, light-filled dining room currently acts as a staging area for a handful of delivery brands that are operated exclusively through Postmates and staffed by a local catering company known for cooking at corporate events for the likes of Nike and Spotify.

Less than a mile south, an Umani Burger location on Broadway is expanding its kitchen to prepare food for Krispy Rice and Sam's Crispy Chicken, two delivery brands developed by SBE, Umani Burger's parent company. With a goal of opening 200 ghost kitchen locations nationwide by the end of 2021, SBE plans to take advantage of underutilized kitchen facilities at its entertainment and hotel properties, according to press materials.

However, tenant turnover at the ghost kitchen commissaries remains consistently high, pointing from a Kitchen Fund report that showed the average ghost kitchen operator needs to generate at least $650,000 in annual sales to break even. By comparison, the average Chipotle store generates just under $400,000 annually from delivery and pickup.

In addition to the commission fees paid to third-party delivery apps, currently capped at 15% in Los Angeles, a ghost kitchen tenant might be charged anywhere from 15% to

30% of its sales in addition to its monthly rent. And if you're operating a food brand owned by someone else? Expect to pay around 15% of sales as a license fee. After subtracting food and labor costs, what remains is an increasingly diminutive slice of the pie.

The cost of entry isn't as low as it seems. Sure, the up-front costs can be lower because there's no physical storefront, which is why some call it a ghost kitchen, but that's also the main problem in the end. If you have no storefront, you have no relationship and trust with the customer and community. They don't know the difference between you and anyone else on an app. You need a presence established, a sign on the road, marketing, and social media presence with lots of promotion. I will dive deeper into all of this further into the book, along with tips and bonuses to add value of your ghost kitchen first-time experience.

Aaron Jones, co-owner of Taco Pete in Compton, was originally drawn to Cloud Kitchen because it offered the chance to expand his family's 50-year-old restaurant brand at a fraction of the price of opening a second location or paying $60,000 to lease a food truck.

Six months into his lease at a commissary space, Jones said he feels the ghost kitchen model is more favorable for businesses with established names, at least when it comes to attracting enough customer attention to run a profitable business.

"If we didn't have our original location, it'd probably be very difficult to make this work... If you're new to the business, or if you're a young chef trying to make a name for yourself, it's really hard to get noticed," Jones said.

Ghost kitchens do offer restaurateurs multiple benefits, including lower real estate costs, such as overhead, property maintenance, cleaning, and other front-of-house related expenses. Smaller staffs, since there are no servers, and delivery can be outsourced. A simplified start-up process, as ghost kitchens have lower setup needs and expenses.

However, ghost kitchens do again have their drawbacks. Some of the noteworthy are: Limited customer interactions, as most ghost kitchens won't ever see their guests in person. As a result, ghost kitchens sacrifice direct customer feedback and control over the dining experience. High delivery costs due to high third-party delivery commission rates. Constrained menu options, since not all foods are best consumed off-premises, like steak or seafood that don't 'travel well.'

Despite these cons, which I have to tell you so you are aware before jumping into this ghost kitchen space headfirst and blind, still the advantages of ghost kitchens are so evident that thousands of them are currently operating around the country. And a global phenomenon, too.

It's no wonder why current and aspiring restaurateurs are looking to open their own ghost kitchen delivery service.

Now, with that being said and you having a clear understanding of what is a ghost kitchen and how it operates along with the pros and cons, let's get into the next chapter: a step-by-step guided process for how to open a ghost kitchen and start capitalizing on the growing demand. God bless.

- Chapter 2 -

"How to Start a Ghost Kitchen"

Start-ups such as Postmates aren't just delivering food, they're opening kitchens, too.

The delivery start-up Postmates approached Los Angeles noodle house Tatsu Ramen with an offer: the start-up would rent a commissary kitchen just west of downtown in an area with a dearth of ramen restaurants. It would supply all the equipment needed to make steaming bowls of ramen. And Tatsu could use it, with no upfront charge, to prepare dishes for delivery.

The catch? Tatsu could use the kitchen only to prep orders for Postmates, and Postmates would take a larger commission from each sale.

"It was a no-brainer for us. It was a low investment on our end, and we could test the market fairly quickly," said William

Khoe, the owner of Tatsu Ramen, which has restaurants in Fairfax and the West Side.

Now, San Francisco Bay Area delivery apps such as Postmates, UberEats, DoorDash, and Caviar used to only be middlemen in the restaurant world. Customers logged onto the apps to find the food they were craving, and the apps would deploy delivery drivers to pick up the meals from restaurants and drop them off at diners' doors. But being the middlemen also meant that they amassed a ton of data about restaurant popularity, consumer preferences, and which neighborhoods are lacking certain cuisines—information that most restaurants struggle to collect on their own.

Armed with this invaluable data, start-ups such as Postmates are reshaping their role in the restaurant industry to be less delivery dispatcher, more business planner.

Before we go further into this book, I want to enlighten the readers that don't know what a restaurateur and a foodie is by definition, because you will hear me use it throughout the book willingly.

A restaurateur is a person who owns or manages a restaurant; the operator or proprietor of a restaurant.

A foodie is a person who enjoys and cares about food very much. A person having an avid interest in the latest food fads. So there you have it. And I definitely admit I do recognize as a foodie myself and the full definition as I mention in the opening chapter of this book, too.

The first actionable step to starting a ghost kitchen is to create a business plan. Write a business plan and source funding. It doesn't matter if the ghost kitchen is an extension of an existing brand or if it's a totally new concept. Every new restaurant needs a business plan.

Experienced restaurateurs know that business plan is the first legitimate step in creating a thriving business. It encourages its writers to think through major topics like funding, financing, and operations before breaking ground on the business.

Restaurateurs can use this restaurant business plan template to start crafting a plan or you can find many custom fit ones online, too.

In addition, most businesses require funding to get off the ground and that includes any ghost kitchens. While expenses may be smaller than a typical restaurant, ghost kitchens can still cost tens or hundreds of thousands of dollars for equipment, a location, proper licenses, marketing, and other purchases for start-up expenses.

Kitchen space can be bought and converted to meet the needs of the restaurant, but this is time-consuming and expensive. The other option is to rent kitchen space, which would involve utilizing an established kitchen for a short period of time.

Companies like The Kitchen Door, Kitchen United, and Cloud Kitchens allow up-and-coming concepts to enter the ghost kitchen market by renting space in licensed commercial kitchens to prepare and sell their food.

Adhere to restaurant regulations. Despite not having a front-of-house, ghost kitchens are subject to the same regulations and licenses that affect restaurants. Preparing and serving food must be done safely and with the proper precautions, which often requires permits. The restaurant permits and licenses needed to legally operate include, but are not limited to, a business license, food service license, employee health permit, seller's permit, resale permit, kitchen management/food management card, which in Arizona was around $37. Check your state listings or neighboring state if you're looking into starting up your ghost kitchen in larger busy cities.

Let's go over the business plan and tips to add value to your venture start-up success. Net profit, gross profit, and deductibles.

You may write a business plan and realize it's not beneficial, then trash it. Regardless if you don't raise money, get a loan, a business plan will help you manage, organize to launch, including needs or what your ghost kitchen doesn't need.

Remember, a great business plan will give you a vivid picture of these following bonus tips.

The vision and purpose of the business, how the business functions/operates, what the business needs, what revenues can be realistically expected, how you compare to competition, how will you promote and market it, how will the business make money, what will you do with those revenues, projection 1 year income and expense, cost from employees.

What will be done once needs are met, what will you do to launch it, strengths or unique talents such as niches of the business, opportunities and threats of the business, 12-month summary of same for years 2 and 3.

However, some business plans are usually no more than 5-10 pages, while others are highly more detailed hundreds of pages. Some try to lure investors, attract friends, colleagues, or family, and convince a banker.

Whereas others only have their business plans interested in the quickest way to make a business profitable. Write down and plan steps to get your ghost kitchen to generate revenue quick as possible (ROI) Return On Investment.

Now, let's move forward into food safety in your ghost kitchen, especially if you are looking into renting a commercial kitchen space like myself.

Without seeing customers day-in and day-out, the focus of the ghost kitchen can quickly become output rather than ensuring the quality and integrity of dishes.

This mindset can be a ghost kitchen's downfall. Food safety and quality should never be overlooked since doing so can cost a restaurant repeat customers and potentially get it shut down. Regulated and inspected as a kitchen, it's your job and ghost kitchen space duty to make sure no microorganism goes out to the public.

Food safety training, safe practices and procedure to your ghost kitchen and all your staff. Here are some more bonus tips to add value to your ghost kitchen initiative. Personal hygiene, ServSafe Food exam and certificate, we will go over it thru my kitchen experience from the sinks, disposing grease and garbage, to the line.

There are three different types of food contamination: physical, biological, and chemical. Physical is foreign objects in food like hair. Biological is like bacteria, viruses, fungi, or parasites are present. Chemical is like cleaning agents, sanitizers, or pesticides enter the food. Remember sanitation and cleaning your ghost kitchen is mandatory daily and first and foremost or else there will be no delivery services, take-out or dining in. No restaurant chain can exist without these proper safety training, practices, and procedures.

ServSafe Food Handler is designed for food service employees who are not in a management position. It certifies that you have basic knowledge in the areas of personal hygiene, cleaning and sanitation, basic food safety, time and temperature, and cross-contamination and allergens. Also cleaning environments in the kitchen space to cook and cut out pest control proactively. It's all about food safety handling.

ServSafe Manager is food manager certifies that you have the knowledge necessary to prevent foodborne illness. It usually requires an exam and fee to get the certificate.

ServSafe Allergens is for those wishing to obtain ServSafe certification needed to pass exam. Allergens course and assessment are offered online, takes about 90 minutes to complete.

Allergen certification is how to deal with people with dietary restrictions or food allergies, like gluten, and cross-contamination. Like a gluten intolerance, maybe use a spoon for the rice or something that contains gluten.

Common food allergies. The big eight in food allergies are foods that cause 90% of all allergic reactions are: peanuts, milk and dairy, wheat and gluten, shellfish, eggs, fish, soy, and tree nuts. Up to 170 additional foods can elicit an allergic response in people.

Start-ups is always scary, risky, not sure if it's going to work. But you have your own will and space to create. Get habits, structures, and processes built. Have clear pick spots where is real growth opportunity. If you love being in the kitchen, get others that love kitchen, too. Form concept and involve people along the way. Help them feel a part of it. Like this is why we doing this and keep them focused. Get community and food community involved, too.

It's hard to get big companies buy in and involved in start-ups. It takes steps in success and a seed needs to grow daily. Push, grind thru it. Don't be afraid to fail, water it. You can always bring in partners, look for partnership to split the cost and work. Remember if cooking and running a kitchen is your passion, push. Define your value, core values, reinforce them over emphasis on your core value. Make sure new people align in values. Your kitchen can only grow if you do. Time management, design thinking, networking, brand building.

Start off by doing prep and getting in there to learn as much as you can. Be willing to be patient with self and the process. You can think you going to come into the space to run it and take over. Be willing to learn more and give your start-up time to grow. Your budget and planning for future growth and to make it to that 5-year food industry goal. Make sure staff can keep up with demand. You shouldn't have to downsize.

What is your mission? To bring your virtual menu to mainstream, to go viral to franchise and get in demand. Social and culture scenes. Look at median income, added personal income. And remember you must do a reality check, add expenses, sales taxes, and utilities. Streamline the process to simplify. The Council for Community and Economic Research you can look up city-by-city comparison of cost online for ghost kitchens. Also U.S. Dept. of State is a list of resources to help you get started. It may be a fee. However, it can help you make an informed choice. Licensing requirements vary by state. For more information and to apply for a peddler's license, contact your city licensing department, too. Some places is slow with ghost kitchen delivery services because of the weather in different parts of the country, at different times of the year where take-out may be slow. Like snowstorms, rainy conditions, tornadoes, monsoons, or hurricanes. So be selective and diligent when choosing cities and locations.

Now, let's fall back in further to the sanitation and food safety importance in your ghost kitchen start-ups.

Sanitary food handling teaches how to properly handle and prepare food. Sanitation procedures teaches you proper sanitation procedures. Importance of food safety teaches you why food safety is so important. Food service accidents, how to avoid some common injuries in a professional kitchen.

Personal cleanliness and health, the importance of personal cleanliness and hygiene in the workplace.

Follow personal cleanliness guidelines for employees in the food service. Understand the importance behind cleanliness in a business in the food service. Compose a cleaning schedule list. Understand correct sanitation.

Personal cleanliness. Many foodborne illnesses are traced to the employees who handle foods. Food service employees should not cough or sneeze into their hands, smoke cigarettes, scratch their heads, touch their faces, or otherwise practice habits that will contaminate their hands and the food they work with. All food service employees should have regular physical examinations by a medical doctor.

Many local laws require blood tests, chest x-rays, and examinations when food service worker is hired, and on a regular basis thereafter. Food service employees who are sick should not report to work. An employee with a cold, cough, open sore, or boil could easily contaminate food. An employee who has been exposed to an infectious disease should consult a doctor before returning to work.

Here are some tips of personal cleanliness guidelines for food service employees. Bathe daily and use deodorant and antiperspirant, shampoo your hair as often as necessary to keep it healthy and clean. Wear it in a simple, easy-to-manage style. Wear clean clothes or uniforms. Keep your fingernails clean, well-trimmed, and free of nail polish. Do not wear excessive makeup or perfume. Do not wear jewelry other than unadorned wedding bands. This guideline is primarily for sanitary reasons, but it also helps protect both you and your jewelry. Wear clean, low-heeled, properly fitting shoes with non-skid soles. The heel and toe should be completely enclosed for sanitation and safety reasons. Don't wear tennis shoes, slippers or sandals.

Always wash your hands with soap and warm water before beginning a new food-handling operation. Your hands should also be washed before returning from the restroom, after touching your face or hair, and after handling soiled articles, including money. Wash hands in hand-washing basins, not preparation or dishwashing sinks. Use disposable towels to dry your hands, not dish towels, aprons or your clothes or uniform.

Employees should wear hair restraints, they should not use hairspray as substitute. Avoid hairpins and barrettes because they can slip out into the food to contaminate. Do not comb your hair, use hairspray, file your nails, or apply makeup in food service areas.

Do not smoke or chew gum in any food production areas. Don't cough or sneeze near food. It is unsanitary to carry used handkerchiefs in your pocket. If needed, disposable tissues should be used and then discarded.

Employee eating habits have an impact on sanitation. Establish and enforce rules about where and when employees can eat. Designate specific areas for employee use, and permit eating only in those areas. Employees should be required to wash their hands after they finish eating.

Now, I will provide a sample cleaning list for your ghost kitchen bonus tips.

Surfaces: Clean counters several times a day. Sanitize at closing. Clean floors daily, after closing. Clean with soap and water. Use a bleach solution weekly. Doorknobs: Germs collect on doorknobs and can be transferred to staff and guests of your ghost kitchen, including delivery pick-up drivers, too. They should frequently be wiped clean.

Restrooms: A male and female employee should be assigned to check the restrooms on a regular basis for cleanliness and the needs for supplies. Wash everything at night by hand or pressure wash with the right cleaning agents and water temps. Bleach should not be used to remove stains on utensils, and it can scratch the enamel coating of the china, and eventually make stains permanent. Turn upside down to air dry overnight for use next day.

Sanitary methods of cleaning small wares are highly important. As well as providing a safety standard, they will give your ghost kitchen establishment an appealing professional safety image. Here are some more helpful bonus tips for cleaning your ghost kitchen.

Pre-soaking: Often, a pre-soaking process is required to properly wash heavily soiled dishware. Remove large quantities of soiled food from dishware with a spatula, brush or other utensil before washing. Inspect dishware during washing and discard cracked, chipped or unusable items in your kitchen.

Sink type: Wash dishware in a sink with at least three or four compartments. If a three-compartment sink is used, the normal process will involve pre-washing, washing, rinsing, and sanitizing. And always follow local and other health codes.

When washing, use the proper type and quantity of dishwashing soap, based on information from the soap's manufacturer or supplier. Provide employees with the proper measuring equipment. Use plastic brushes with firm bristles to wash dishware. Do not use dish cloths, dish mops, or soft sponges, they are very difficult to keep clean. Do not use metal cleaning brushes, because they can leave metal slivers in or on items being washed. Wash glasses with a glassware brush.

Keep water hot. The normal order of washing is as follows: glassware, flatware, dishes, trays, and pots and pans. Frequently drain wash water and refill with clean, fresh, hot water.

Rinse racks: After they are washed, glasses, cups, and bowls should be placed loosely in the racks so that rinse water will reach all surfaces. For the same reason, dishes, trays, and pots and pans should not be crowded on the rinsing racks, irregardless on how small your ghost kitchen space is to work with.

Sanitizing: Remove all detergent from dishes before placing them in the rinse sink. Fill rinsing sink with clean water at approximately 180°F (82°C) if sanitizing with hot water. If sanitizing with chemicals, it's possible to sanitize with water at a much lower temperature. Remember that different chemicals may call for different temperatures. Always check the manufacturer's instructions. Change rinse water frequently. All for commercial kitchen's dishwashing procedure.

Properly sanitizing dishware: There are two ways to properly sanitize dishware washed manually. Hot water: Water must be at least 180°F (82°C) to sanitize dishware. To raise water to that temperature, you need a booster heater or an electrical heating element that can be immersed directly in the water. Since employees cannot remove items from 180-degree water with their hands, they must use tongs or other devices.

Chemicals: It is frequently more practical to use a chemical sanitizing agent to sanitize dishes. If chemicals are used, the water does not need to be excessively hot. Use proper chemical sanitizing agents in the correct amount. Determine the quantities to use, and provide appropriate training and measuring utensils to employees.

Many foodborne illnesses are caused by poor personal cleanliness by employees working in the food service. This means it is vital for a business in the food service to have guidelines for its employees to follow in regards to cleanliness. A cleaning schedule should be followed to ensure proper sanitation with the establishment, and to develop a great public image.

Sanitation procedures: Employees should avoid leaving inventory on the loading dock as otherwise perishable goods may get spoiled through bacterial growth. Instead, count inventory immediately and store it in its proper area, such as a refrigerator, freezer, or dry storage, not on the floor, as it is easily contaminated by dirt. Food should always be stored in its proper area.

Employees should avoid storing food against a wall, there should be at least 2 inches between the wall and food. This is to ensure proper air circulation. Leftover food should not be left outside as this encourages contamination. Food should be refrigerated as soon as possible. Food should not be held in temperatures between 45°F (7°C) and 140°F (60°C). Food should be stored in a refrigerator as soon as possible to avoid contamination.

Employees should not refreeze food, as this decreases the quality of the food substantially and increases the bacteria count. The food should be used completely, or stored after it's cooked. Food should always be cooked completely, heat it without interruption. If food looks suspicious it should not be tasted, it should be thrown out. This is to preserve the employees' health.

Employees also should never eat unwashed fruits or vegetables, or open cans which have not had the tops washed as this may cause contamination. Food particles should not be left on equipment, glasses, flatware or dishware. This may cause contamination. All equipment should be inspected for cleanliness before use.

Cracked or chipped glasses or dishware should not be used, as bacteria can grow in the cracks. Employees should never handle glasses by the rim, utensils by the eating portion or the tops of plates, as they may transfer bacteria to the dishware. Proper handling etiquette is to touch dishes only by the edge, cups by the handles, glasses near the base and utensils by the base.

Soiled dishes should never be placed on the same tray with food that is to be served, as this may cause contamination. Instead separate trays should be used to clear the table. Employees should never allow food to stand on the service counter as cooling food increases chances of bacterial growth. Instead it should be served at once. Employees should never sit on counters or tables, or lean on tables as contaminants on clothing will be transferred to tables.

Hair should not be worn loose, as hair falls into food and causes contamination, and is also extremely unappetizing. Hairnets should be worn. Employees should keep their hands away from their faces and hair, and out of their pockets, due to the possibility of contamination. If any of these things must be done, hands must be washed thoroughly straight away. Never chew gum or anything of a similar nature as this can spread infection.

Never carry cash, debit cards, or pens in your mouth or put a pen or pencil in your hair as these actions spread infection. The cash, debit cards should be carried in hand and ink pens in your pocket. Especially dealing with take-out or in-house dining to your ghost kitchen as an option.

Sneezing, yawning, or coughing should be avoided as these actions spread infection. If unavoidable, make sure not to face food or guests and cover your mouth and ensure hands are washed.

Do not spit, this spreads disease. Do not eat or nibble on the job, or eat from bus trays or soiled dishes. Eat at designated break times and wash hands thoroughly when finished. Never smoke on duty. As well as spreading disease, this can spread the nicotine virus. Smoke in designated areas during breaks and wash hands thoroughly afterwards.

Never use your apron as a towel, a dirty apron will contaminate clean hands. Instead use disposable towels. Employees should never work with dirty hands, as it increases the risk of contamination. Wash hands using warm, soapy water. Lather well and rinse with clear water. Dry hands with disposable towels.

Never handle clean dishes if hands have not been cleaned after touching soiled dishes, as contamination from soiled dishes may occur. Ensure hands are washed thoroughly between these two stages. Employees should never pick up food with hands, as infection can spread from the skin. Proper serving gloves should be used. Employees should not wear soiled clothes into work, as they can harbor infection. A clean uniform and apron should be worn.

Avoid excessive jewelry, as food particles can collect on it and cause contamination. Wear minimum of jewelry, only wedding band, or none. Do not arrive at work needing a bath, as this may cause bacterial contamination. Bathe and use deodorant daily.

Employees should never use the same knife and cutting board for meats and vegetables without washing, as salmonella and other very small organisms can spread if this is done. Instead use a different knife and board or else wash and sanitize.

Do not report to work if sick, as this increases the chances of spreading the illness. Call in sick, so that a replacement may be organized. Do not work with exposed wounds, as this will increase the risk of infecting the wound and spreading the infection. Always keep wounds covered with proper type of bandage. Do not report to work if your healthcare has expired, to help prevent the spread of communicable disease, tuberculosis, and venereal disease. The expiration date should be kept track of and renewed immediately.

Never wash hands in sinks used to prepare food as this may contaminate the food. Instead use the designated hand-washing sink. Employees should never taste food using their finger, as food may be contaminated by saliva. A tasting spoon should be used, and used only once. Food should never be reserved, as the handling of food by guests can spread disease. Food should be thrown away, and an excess of rolls, etc., should be avoided. I do a burn/sample tray or dish and

Saran Wrap it, date it, and freeze it just in case any sickness the food can be tested and examined.

Pork should never be served rare, to prevent trichinosis. Always cook pork until fully cooked to kill trichina organisms. Racks of glasses should not be left bowl-side up as airborne illness can collect up. Instead store glassware inverted. Food should never be stored in an open container, as airborne particles can contaminate foods. Always store food in sealed containers.

Food that is prepped already should not be left out, as airborne illness can collect up and airborne particles can contaminate foods. Prepare food immediately prior to cooking/serving.

Employees should never dry silverware, glasses, utensils or cooking equipment with a towel, as this increases the chance of infection. They should be let air dry, or dry in a dishwasher machine's cycle.

Garbage should not be stored with food, as this may cause bacterial contamination. There should be a proper place for each of these.

Proper food handling is more a matter of developing a proper attitude than memorizing an extensive list of do's and don'ts. If you and your employees understand the need to be careful with food and know basic sanitation principles, many of the specific rules become a matter of common sense. The first step in proper food handling is simply making it clear to everyone that sanitation is a priority when purchasing, receiving, storing, preparing, and serving foods.

Learning outcomes: Know what the difference is between inspection and grading. Know what to expect, and what is irregular when receiving foods from a supplier. Be able to store foods at the correct temperature upon delivery. Understand the importance of thawing foods in the proper manner. Know a number of guidelines to follow when storing foods. Be able to prepare food while adhering to guidelines that are significantly important to food sanitation. Have knowledge of the different temperatures required by different food types.

Purchasing food: Restaurant/kitchen personnel should only purchase food that is wholesome and suitable to eat. Food should be obtained from commercial sources that comply with all applicable local, regional, and national sanitation laws. Generally, meat and poultry products shipped from other countries should be inspected by agents from the Department of Agriculture to make sure these products are suitable for consumption.

Inspection is done at the processing plants in the USA to make sure that meat and poultry products have the proper quality; the plant is clean; proper procedures are used by the plant's employees. Purchasers should be aware of the difference between inspection and grading.

Inspection refers to an official examination of food to determine whether or not it is wholesome. Grading refers to the process of analyzing food relative to specific, defined standards in order to assess its quality. Inspection is often required by law, but grading is optional.

Many purchasers prefer to buy graded products because they know those products have met specific quality standards. This is one reason producers are willing to pay to have their fruits, cheese, vegetables, and other products graded. Purchasers should be aware graded at the processing plants; improper handling by delivery or restaurant personnel can adversely affect quality.

Receiving foods: All incoming food should be checked to make sure they meet quality standards stated in the operation's purchase specifications. Employees who receive American meats and poultry for the operation should look for the USDA "Inspected & Passed" labels.

I'll give you some additional receiving food products bonus tips.

Look at the condition of the delivery vehicle. Does the interior look clean? Is it an open-bed truck or an enclosed truck? The chance that products may be contaminated is greater with an open-bed truck.

Carefully inspect every case that appears damaged; there is a possibility that the food within may be contaminated. Check all deliveries for evidence of insect or rodent contamination. Check incoming products for unusual or foul odors. Such odors generally mean a problem exists. Don't accept frozen foods that feel partially or completely thawed, or appear to be spoiled.

Storing foods: Food should be stored as soon as possible after receiving. Keep stored foods covered, as uncovered food may dry out or absorb odors. It is also possible for debris or other objects to fall into uncovered food from storage shelves above. Store frozen foods in their original containers because these containers are usually moisture- and vapor-proof.

Store staples such as flour, cornmeal, and rice in rust-proof and corrosion-resistant containers with tight-fitting lids. Do not use metal containers, they are hard to clean, sanitize, and maintain. Keep stored food away from walls and dripping pipes. Place food on slotted shelves that are at least two inches away from the wall and six inches off the floor.

Recommended refrigerated storage practices: All cooked food or other products removed from original container must be enclosed in clean, sanitized, covered containers and identified. Do not store packaged food in contact with water or undrained ice. Check refrigerator thermometers regularly.

Recommended temperatures are as follows. Produce: 45°F (7°C) or below. Dairy and meat: 40°F (4°C) or below. Seafood: 30°F (-1°C) or below.

Store large pieces of meat and all foods in a way that permits free circulation of cool air on all surfaces. Do not store food directly on floor or base.

Schedule cleaning of equipment and refrigerated storage rooms at regular intervals. Date all merchandise upon receipt, which I usually do or have ghost kitchen staff do with a black or red permanent marker. And you also rotate inventory on a "first-in, first-out" basis. Check fruits and vegetables daily for spoilage. Store dairy products separately from foods with a strong odor. Store fish apart from other food products.

Establish a preventive maintenance program for equipment. Facilitate air circulation and floor cleaning. Don't line shelves with paper or other materials because this will block airflow. All shelves must be clean. Food that cannot be stored on shelves because of size or bulk should be stored on easily movable dollies or skids, not on the floor.

Even if it is in containers, food should never be stored on the floor because these containers may be placed on kitchen counters to be opened and emptied; this would allow soil on the bottom of the containers to contaminate the counter.

Also remember in no kitchen or restaurant is a such thing of this 5-second rule where food is safe to consume if it hits the ground for under 5 seconds. If absolutely anything from food to cooking utensils hit the floor, throw it out or sanitize it. Don't risk cross-contamination and getting people sick or your ghost kitchen shut down.

Recommended temperatures in refrigerated storage areas vary with the type of food being stored. Freezer temperatures should be 0°F (-18°C) or below.

Food products not requiring refrigeration or freezing should be stored in clean, cool, and moisture-free areas that are well-ventilated and free from rodents and insects. Temperatures for dry food products should be between 50°F (10°C) and 70°F (21°C); relative humidity should range from 50% to 60%. Products that seem spoiled or unusable should be thrown away, but be sure that employees notify you first!

Issue food to preparation or service areas on a first-in, first-out (FIFO) basis. In other words, products that are in storage the longest should be used first. Do not ever worry about holding stocks of inventory in your ghost kitchen to risk getting people sick. Remember before storing a product, mark the date the inventory was received on the package or container it came in. This will help with stock rotation. Inspect storage areas often. Do not keep poisons, toxic substances, or cleaning materials in food storage areas.

Preparing foods: Basic sanitation procedures should always be followed when working with and around food. Hand washing: Keeping hands clean during food preparation is a must. Wash hands for at least 20-30 seconds. The use of disposable gloves is often practical. Tools and surfaces: Be sure to clean food preparation tools and other equipment properly. Sanitize contact surfaces between every food-processing task.

Cans: Wash the tops of cans before opening them. Do not use cans that have swelling at the tops or bottoms, or those with dents along the side seams. Swelling could mean that germs have contaminated the product, dents along the side seams may indicate the can's seal is broken. If canned products have unusual or unfamiliar odor, or if the contents seem foamy or milky, don't use them.

Do's and Don'ts: Wash all raw fruits and vegetables thoroughly before preparation or serving. Be especially careful when handling and preparing meat, eggs, fish, shellfish, and other foods high in protein. Do not use meats that smell strange or have slimy surfaces. Generally, any type of food that appears moldy, cloudy, or that has a strange smell should be discarded, too. Do not taste foods, since this test proves nothing and can make you ill.

Freezing and thawing: Never leave food out overnight to thaw. Potentially hazardous foods should be thawed in one of the following ways:

In refrigerated units. Under running water at a temperature of 70°F (21°C) or below. In a microwave oven if the product will be immediately transferred to other cooking equipment as part of cooking process, for example when steaks are charbroiled from their frozen state.

Do not refreeze thawed products. Freezing, thawing, and refreezing can create sanitation problems and destroy food quality.

Preparing foods: Some foods require a higher temperature before serving. The center of poultry, poultry stuffings, stuffed meats, and stuffing containing meat should be heated to 165°F (74°C), pork to 150°F (66°C). On the other hand, rare roast beef and rare beefsteak need to be heated only to 130°F (54°C).

Meat and poultry temperatures should be checked with a cooking thermometer. Prepare perishable foods as close to serving time as possible. To kill any germs that may be present, all foods should normally be heated to at least 140°F (60°C) in the center of the food mass. Keep cold foods refrigerated until serving begins or during service. Many ghost kitchens have refrigerators where prepared foods can be kept until service.

However, pre-prepare foods, the dangers! A common problem in many food service operations involves holding hot foods that are prepared in advance of service. Casseroles, stews, gravies, and other products high in protein are often kept in a hot-water bath at lukewarm temperatures for long periods of time. If germs get into these products, conditions are ideal for food poisoning or infection. Protein foods must be kept above 140°F (60°C) or below 145°F (70°C) or they should not be kept at all.

Now, let's do a sanitary food handling summary. Know what to look for when receiving food. Does the delivery vehicle look sanitary? Is the delivery case damaged? Does it look like there is insect/rodent contamination? Are there foul odors? Do the frozen goods seem partially thawed?

When purchasing food, it should be ensured that the commercial sources comply with all applicable local, regional, and national sanitation laws. Incoming foods should be checked to ensure that they meet quality standards stated in the operation's purchase specifications. I'll provide a basic overview of food safety cleanliness.

Freezer temperatures should be 0°F (-18°C) or below. Temperatures for dry food products and storage should be between 50°F (10°C) and 70°F (21°C); relative humidity should range from 50% to 60%. When preparing foods, make sure to follow basic sanitation procedures. Keep hands clean. Keep equipment clean.

When thawing frozen foods make sure to do so: In refrigerated units. Under running water at a temperature of 70°F (21°C) or below. In a microwave oven if the product will be immediately transferred to other cooking equipment as part of the cooking process. For example, when steaks are charbroiled from their frozen state. Upon receiving food, make sure it is stored correctly. Store frozen foods in original containers. Store flour and rice, etc., in rust-proof and corrosion-resistant containers with tight-fitting lids.

Recommended refrigeration temperatures: produce 45°F (7°C) or below. Dairy and meat 40°F (4°C) or below. Seafood 30°F (-1°C) or below.

Importance of food safety. Learning outcomes. Know the cause of unsafe food and how to avoid carrying them out yourself. Know the different causes of food poisoning, and which foods they affect. Know how food infections are caused, their symptoms, and which foods they affect.

Causes of unsafe food: There are numerous reasons that food could be compromised and become unsafe. By knowing these reasons, it is easier for you to avoid them.

Chemical poisoning: Cleaning agents, pesticides, and other toxic substances must be kept away from food. Fruits and vegetables should be washed thoroughly before use. Canned food must be removed from opened cans and stored in other containers. Do not use rusted pots and pans or cooking utensils.

Germs: Germs are too small to see without a microscope. Not all of them are harmful; some are beneficial and useful. We need them to make bread, cheese, wine, and sauerkraut. Some are used to manufacture.

Salmonella (SAM) poisoning: Eating improperly cooked food containing this organism. Caused by contact with fecal material, most from rodents. In meat, poultry, eggs, baked goods with cream filling.

Clostridium perfringens: Eating food contaminated by food handlers or insects. Found in meats, poultry, soups, gravy and sauces made with meat or poultry. Strep: Eating foods contaminated by coughing, sneezing, dust, dirt from clothing or contaminated air in the ghost kitchen facility.

Trichinosis: Eating contaminated pork meat or products. Tuberculosis: Eating food handled by carriers of the disease. Transmitted in milk or milk products.

Food infections: Salmonellosis. The most common form of food infection. SAM germs live in the intestinal tract of people, hogs, and chickens. Foods especially susceptible are ground beef, pork, poultry, fish, eggs, egg products, and cream fillings. Occurs within 12-48 hours. Symptoms include abdominal pain, diarrhea, fever, vomiting, and chills.

Clostridium perfringens: Germs found everywhere: medications, and some are necessary in our body to help with digestion. However, some germs are harmful and dangerous. These include bacteria, viruses, molds, and parasites.

The most dangerous germs are the ones which prefer the foods we like: meat, poultry, fish, eggs, and baked foods with cream fillings. They need moisture and favorable temperatures between 45°F (7°C) and 140°F (60°C) in order to multiply rapidly and provoke foodborne illnesses.

Allergies: Some people have allergies that could be fatal. The most known are tree nuts and shellfish.

There are two basic types of foodborne illnesses: Food poisoning. Illness caused by germ-produced poisons. Staphylococcus poisoning. Botulism. Salmonella (SAM) poisoning. Clostridium perfringens. Strep. Trichinosis. Tuberculosis.

Food infections. Illness caused by germs in the food. Salmonellosis. Clostridium perfringens.

Food poisoning. Staphylococcus poisoning. Eating food infected by careless food handlers with germs from cuts, sneezing or coughing around food. Found in cream and custard dishes, meat, poultry, ham, and meat salads.

Botulism. Eating food containing poison from bacteria in canned food not properly prepared. Like meat, fish, corn and beans. Also in the soil, in dust, and in the intestinal tracts of people and animals. Infects soups, gravies, and stews kept lukewarm in deep containers for a long time. Occurs within 8-12 hours. Symptoms are abdominal pain and diarrhea.

Food safety summary: Avoid chemical poisoning by keeping utensils sanitary and maintained. Keeping toxic substances away from foods. Not leaving food in opened tins. Washing fruits and vegetables. Keeping foods stored at temperatures less than 45°F (7°C) or higher than 140°F (60°C) will help avoid germs from multiplying and causing foodborne illnesses. Allergies can be fatal, it is important to be aware of allergens on a menu.

Hand-washing: It is widely recognized that hands are a potential source of microbiological and chemical contamination.

Food handlers, if poorly trained and managed, possibly the greatest risk of contamination; in short, they may unwittingly poison foods and, yes, consumers. Frequent hand-washing and good personal hygiene practices will significantly minimize the risk of product contamination.

The company must provide an adequate number of washbasins at suitable locations designated for hand-washing at the ghost kitchen facility you choose to partner with. Washbasins need to have a supply of hot and cold running water or suitably temperature-controlled of appropriate microbiological and chemical quality. A sufficient quantity of appropriate materials for cleaning hands needs to be available at all times. These materials should be appropriate and suitable for use in a food preparation area: unscented soaps or proprietary cleansers, for example. You need to provide for the hygienic drying of hands.

Any materials used for hand-drying must be disposed of without risk of contamination to food products. The ghost kitchen facilities for washing and preparation of food need to be separate from the hand-washing kitchen facilities, and must not be used for hand-washing. Food handlers should use these following methods to ensure hands are appropriately clean.

Hand-washing how-to: Wet hands with warm running water and apply liquid soap or use a clean soap bar. Rub hands vigorously for at least 20 seconds, giving a special attention to the backs of the hands, wrists, between the fingers, and under the fingernails. Rinse hands well while leaving the water running. Dry hands with a clean single-use disposable towel or air drier. Where a disposable towel is used, dispose of it without risk of contamination to the food products. When turning off the water, if it's not automatically done, use dry hands or a clean disposable towel.

Verification: Since hand-washing is critically important for the microbiological safety of food, the person responsible for food safety within the ghost kitchen should monitor this activity carefully. You must watch your employees' hand-washing activities on a fairly regular but non-predetermined basis to assess their compliance with the defined requirements. You may also have to do occasional visual checks on the cleanliness of hands. Checks should be carried out and focused on risk periods, such as after toilet visits and shift changes.

Pests are animals that live in or on food, such as rodents and insects. Pests in food production facilities or kitchen are regarded as a serious hazard and risk to health; they not only can contaminate food with foreign bodies such as feces and hair, but they also may carry fatal diseases. You must cover the requirements for effective control and management of pest control, prevention control of pests, and monitoring.

Pest objectives are: Explain the hazards posed by specific food pests and the controls required to reduce the risk. Explain the preferred habitat of relevant invading pests in your particular kitchen facility. Explain the environmental, physical, and chemical methods of preventing and controlling pest infestations in your ghost kitchen facility. Explain the system used to monitor the effectiveness of pest controls and define corrective actions that must be taken. Design a system to minimize the risk of pest-infestation of the product and the kitchen facility by inspecting and controlling raw materials and making sure the facility is always clean, and that it maintains specific control measures. Operate a system to minimize the risk of pest infestation of the product and the kitchen facility by inspecting and controlling raw materials, and making sure the facility is always clean, and that it maintains specific control measures.

As a person responsible for food safety within the facility/ kitchen, you must develop systems to ensure and monitor that the staff is fully aware of and uses good practices to control pests. Any system will have to be clearly and concisely documented and communicated effectively to appropriate staff within the company.

It is important to work closely with key kitchen or company staff to ensure they clearly understand the importance of such systems and how they can influence effective compliance. As the responsibility for food safety rests with you, direct verification of systems is extremely important for basic level requirements. You should personally systematically monitor activities on a regular basis and record your findings.

Pests are attracted to food premises since they are an ideal habitat in which to live and reproduce. Since pests pose a significant health risk, pest control is extremely important. Inadequate control can lead to pest infestation and serious consequences to consumer health.

Besides potential health risks, pest infestation will inevitably lead to significant waste and, therefore, commercial loss. The loss caused by pest infestation of raw materials or the finished product can be large.

Food products are at high risk of contamination if control measures are not in place. Pests are carriers of food poisoning microorganisms and viruses. Pests can also contaminate food with hair, fur, droppings/urine, eggs, dead bodies.

Certain pests, rodents in particular, can also cause significant damage to a facility kitchen by, for example, chewing through electrical wires and causing fires.

There are many different types of pests that can pose a risk to human health or the commercial viability of your company. These include: rats, mice, insects—cockroaches, flies, ants, stored product pests, larder beetles, weevils, flour moths, reptiles—lizards, birds, animals attracted by pests, notably cats and dogs.

Pests require certain conditions to survive and reproduce: shelter, food, water, and security. As a food safety manager, you must understand what conditions allow pests to survive and reproduce. If you aren't fully aware, your business will suffer contamination and loss that may make the business no longer sustainable.

Prevention: Once pests have entered your factory, it is difficult to control and totally eliminate them, particularly if there is an infestation. You must prevent their invading your ghost kitchen facility! Preventing any and all ingression of pests will be commercially more cost-effective than continually eliminating pest infestation. The control of prevention of ingression of pests requires proofing the premises, monitoring for signs of infestation, practicing good hygiene.

Effective proofing of your kitchen facility premises is the preferred method for control of pests. Doors and windows pose the highest risk of ingression. Yes, a door and window closure policy should be introduced. Other methods may need to be considered: fine mesh screens for windows and doors, self-closing mechanisms on doors, and plastic curtains on internal and external door openings.

Rodents can enter a facility through the smallest of openings, so any gap under doors should be covered with a metal plate. In New York we say a rat can squeeze into a dime-size hole; long as it can fit their heads through, the body will squeeze thru, too, because its spine is flexible.

To prevent flying insects, reptiles, or birds, any holes or openings in the fabrication of the factory must be filled with mortar or covered with metal/plastic sheets or mesh.

As the food safety manager of your ghost kitchen, you must make sure all staff members are aware of signs of pest infestation and possible entry points. They should also be aware of the importance of reporting the presence of any possible infestation right away. Signs to look for are: live animals, dead animals, droppings, smell, eggs, webbing, piles of debris, holes in fabrication, larvae/pupae, damaged packaging, smears/discoloration of walls.

Prevention methods should protect you from the ingression of pests; however, it is a good practice to ensure there are control measures in place to minimize the risk of pest infestation in your kitchen. As a food safety manager, you have a responsibility to ensure control measures are in place. There are two types of pest control: physical and chemical. Both types are designed to control specific types of pests, but by their very nature they should be correctly used since they themselves could pose a risk to your product or staff.

Physical means of control is usually the preferred option. By their very nature, physical means of control are not always 100% effective. A point that should be very seriously considered. In the event of a significant infestation, physical controls cannot cope with the numbers of pests, so alternative methods of elimination must be considered. Typical physical control methods include: electric fly killers, rodent traps, sticky fly strips, curtains, bird screens, and pheromone traps.

Since several of these methods will actually kill pests, you should consider the location and placement of control mechanisms such as electric fly killers and sticky fly traps in order to avoid possible product contamination.

Chemical control measures are much more effective than physical control methods. However, chemical substances do pose possible risks to staff, so their use should be frequently and carefully controlled and monitored. Chemical substances also pose a risk to food contamination, so they should also be used only under controlled and monitored conditions. Because of the risks involved, it is good practice to employ a professional to carry out chemical pest control. Chemical control includes rodenticides, insecticides, and fumigates.

Now, let's get into the role of management. About the roles and responsibilities of a manager. Learning outcomes from knowing what is expected of you as a ghost kitchen manager. Understanding and being able to implement the "lead by example" concept. Know the importance of training your staff correctly. Understand the procedure of accident reports.

Know the importance of inspections for the consistency of sanitation standards.

Although all members of the food service staff are members of the operations, sanitation, and safety team, the development of sanitation and safety programs really begins with a commitment from kitchen management. Managers have the ultimate responsibility for developing, implementing, and monitoring the property's sanitation and safety efforts.

The roles of the manager include: Incorporating sanitation and safety practices into operating procedures. Ensuring that sanitation and safety concerns take priority over convenience. Training employees in sanitary and safe work procedures. Conducting sanitation and safety inspections. Completing accident reports, assisting in investigations, and doing whatever is necessary to ensure that problems are quickly corrected.

When necessary, assisting in treatment and seeking medical assistance for injured employees or guests. Reporting needed repairs or maintenance, changes in work procedures, or other conditions that are potential problems. Conducting sanitation and safety meetings. Urging the active participation of all staff members in solving sanitation and safety problems.

In the United States, OSHA (Occupational Safety & Health Administration) regulations and state worker's compensations laws require that accidents that occur in the workplace be reported. It will be good practice to fill out a report in case of an incident/accident and keep the record. It should be available in case of investigation by the authorities or insurance company.

Required information in a report includes: who was involved/hurt, when, where, and how with details. What was the reaction to injury and what measures have been taken to avoid similar injuries happening in the future?

Inspections are usually at the heart of management's effort to ensure that sanitation and safety procedures are consistently followed. You can develop inspection forms or checklists that focus attention on equipment, facilities, food handling practices, and/or food service employees.

Persons with special knowledge—insurance representatives, state or local fire inspectors, and so on—can help you create these checklists. How often you make sanitation and safety inspections depends, in part, on how well your property measures up during the first inspection. A complete inspection should be made at least monthly. However, if necessary you should also conduct daily inspections of specific workstation areas or equipment.

A primary reason to conduct sanitation and safety inspections is to correct potentially dangerous conditions. Corrective measures should be taken promptly! If time must lapse before a problem is corrected, inform employees of any possible hazards and alert upper management that has been found and steps are being taken to correct it.

After an inspection is completed, inspection forms and checklists should be filed for later reference. Looking back at earlier forms and checklists can give you an indication of the long-range effectiveness of your sanitation and safety programs. Also the forms are evidence of your efforts to maintain a sanitary and safe food and beverage operation.

Management commitment is a very important aspect of an operation's sanitation and safety team. The more committed and active management are in regards safety and sanitation, the more the rest of the food service kitchen staff will respond.

Remember, managers should train employees in sanitary, safe work procedures.

They should try and ensure that sanitation and safety practices are incorporated into operating procedures. They should carry out inspections, once a month at least. Inspections are central to management's effort to ensure that sanitation and safety procedures are consistently followed.

Next let's dive into food service accidents that can occur during business hours of your ghost kitchen. Food service accident learning outcomes. Be able to protect employees and others such as guests. Know how to avoid burns. Know how to avoid muscle strains and falls. Know how to avoid cuts. Know certain precautions for avoiding equipment accidents. Be able to lessen the danger of fire. Know the importance of first aid training. Know how the Heimlich maneuver is performed in theory. Make sure that one only performs the Heimlich maneuver if they have received first aid training.

Burns: Many accidents in ghost kitchen food service operations result in burns. These bonus tips will teach you actions that can be taken to prevent burns, and the importance of burn prevention in the ghost kitchen workplace.

Gas: Follow recommended procedures when using any cooking equipment or when lighting gas equipment. Be prepared! Plan ahead. Always have a place prepared for hot pans before removing them from a range or oven. Use correct handling equipment. Use dry pothandlers; a wet or damp potholder can cause a steam burn. Never use an apron, towel, or dish cloth. Don't reach into hot ovens; use a puller or other proper tool. Boiling water: Don't use pans with loose handles, they can break off, or round bottoms, the pans may tip. Be careful with steam. Don't fill pots, pans, or kettles too full. Open pots carefully by raising the back of their lids so steam will escape away from you. Be careful with splashes. Stir food carefully with long-handled spoons or paddles; avoid splattering and splashing.

Fire: Know how to put out fires. If food catches on fire, spread salt or baking soda on the flame; do not use water. Know how to use fire extinguishers properly, which directions should always be on them, and other safety equipment.

General guidelines: Allow equipment to cool before cleaning it. Prohibit horseplay. Be careful when pouring coffee and other hot liquids. Use caution around heat lamps.

Muscle strains and falls: Muscle strains can be avoided by taking care and using the correct lifting method. Next to traffic accidents, falls kill more people than any other kind of accident. Most falls are not from high places, but are slips or trips at floor level. Precautions for avoiding muscle strains and falls bonus tips outlines how to prevent slipping on a personal level.

Lifting correctly: To avoid muscle strains, always have a firm footing before attempting to lift a heavy object. Keep your back straight; do not bend forward or sideways. Bend your knees to pick up low objects and lift with your legs, not your back. Kitchen employees should not try to carry too many items at one time or items that are too heavy for them. When carrying a heavy load, ask for help or use a cart.

Spills: Keep floors clean and dry at all times. Wipe up spills immediately. Use "slip-resistant" floor waxes and use "caution" or "wet floor" signs when appropriate. Keep floors in good repair. Keep hazardous objects such as boxes, mops, and brooms off floors. Replace loose or upturned floor tiles as soon as they are noticed. Repair cracked or worn stair treads.

Corrective footwear: Wear properly-fitting shoes with low heels and non-skid soles. Never wear worn-out shoes, thin-soled shoes, slippers, high heels, tennis shoes, or sandals. The heel and toe of the shoe should be completely enclosed. Keep shoestrings tied to prevent tripping. Walk, don't run, and use caution when going through swinging doors. Don't reach. Use a sturdy stepladder if it is necessary to reach high places.

Pay attention to doorways. Make sure that entrances and exits are clean and safe. This includes removing mud if the ghost kitchen property is located in an area where there is a potential problem with rain. Keep floor mats or other protective devices clean and in good condition. Lighting: Keep any areas in which employees must work or walk well-lit; pay special attention to exterior areas and steps where accidents are more likely to occur.

Now, cuts are constant hazards for food preparation employees. I'd like to share bonus tips how to properly cut food in a safe manner.

Chopping: Employees must be alert when using knives, slicers, or similar equipment. There are many common guidelines for using knives. Always place food to be cut on a table or a cutting board. Cut away from your body; the food item should be firmly grasped and sliced by cutting downward. When chopping food with a knife, hold the food with your free hand and keep the point of the knife on the block. Dull knives cause more problems than sharp knives because dull knives require employees to exert more pressure, and slippage problems are more likely to occur.

General care: Discard or repair knives with loose handles. Don't leave knives on the edge of a counter, push them back so they cannot fall on the floor or on someone's foot. Don't try to catch a falling knife. Never play with knives or use them as substitutes for screwdrivers or can openers. Don't use knives to open cardboard cartons; use the proper container-opening tool.

Cleaning: Cuts can also occur when knives or other sharp tools are washed. For this reason, all sharp tools should be washed separately. Never place knives or other sharp tools in sinks filled with soapy water; clean all sharp tools with caution. Use a folded heavy cloth and work slowly and carefully from the center of the blade to the outside cutting edge. When cleaning a slicer, make sure the blade of the slicer is in the position recommended for cleaning. Unplug the unit and refer to the manufacturer's operating and maintenance manual for specific cleaning instructions.

Broken glass: Minimizing the use of glass in the kitchen can help prevent cuts. Any broken glass should be cleaned up immediately with a broom and dustpan, not your fingers.

If glass is broken in a dishwasher, drain the dishwasher and pick up the glass with a damp cloth. Always place broken glass or china in a separate refuse container.

General safety guidelines: Keep knives, cleavers, saws, and other sharp tools in racks or special drawers when not in use. Use the correct size cutting tools and make sure they have the proper blade. Use safety guards and any other safety items provided on equipment. Use caution when operating slicers and other electric cutting tools. When using sharpening steels, be sure there is a finger guard between the handles and the steel.

Equipment accidents: Safety precautions should be used whenever kitchen employees work with equipment. Instructions: Don't take shortcuts when operating potentially hazardous food service equipment; always follow the manufacturer's instructions carefully. Place the instructions on or near equipment so that employees can refer to them. Procedures: Train employees how to use, maintain, and clean equipment. New employees should be carefully supervised to ensure that proper procedures are followed. When possible, disconnect equipment from power sources before cleaning.

Maintenance: Properly maintain equipment. Improper maintenance can lead to unsafe working conditions. Conduct regular and detailed equipment inspections with maintenance personnel or representatives from the equipment supply company.

Regulations: Make sure all gas connections conform with applicable regulations. Ensure that all electrical equipment and connections conform to national, state, and local electrical code requirements. Electrical equipment should, where applicable, bear the Underwriters Laboratories seal of approval.

Electrical equipment: Carefully follow the manufacturer's instructions whenever operating electrical equipment. Always unplug electrical equipment before cleaning it. Never touch metal sockets and electrical equipment when your hands are wet or you are standing on a wet floor. Practice preventive maintenance. A qualified electrician should inspect all electrical equipment, wiring, switches, etc., on a regular basis.

Fire: Another potential accident cause in kitchen food service operations is fire. The following precautions can help lessen the danger of fire. Simple measures properly clean and maintain cooking equipment and exhaust hoods/filters.

For sanitation as well as safety reasons, limit smoking to restricted areas.

Fire extinguishers: Be sure there is adequate fire extinguishing equipment on hand. Personnel should know where it is located and how to use it. Consult local fire authorities about the purchase, use, and inspection of fire-extinguishing equipment. Local ordinances frequently require special fire-extinguishing equipment under ventilation filters. Regardless of the type, dry chemical, carbon dioxide, or chemicals in special solutions, this equipment can only be effective if it is professionally designed, installed, and maintained.

Fire detection: Consider using fire detection devices. These may be specialized equipment items that can detect smoke, flames, and/or heat. In the future, consider using automatic sprinkler systems. They are a very effective way to control fires.

Emergency procedures: Kitchen employees should know where all emergency exits are located, and fire drills should be conducted. Contact local fire department for specific help in designing emergency procedures. Make sure all doors to the property open out and that fire exits are kept clear at all times. Fire department telephone numbers should be located near telephones.

First aid: Immediately after an accident occurs, first aid is the primary concern. It is very important that someone trained in first aid apply treatment. People without first aid training normally should only undertake common-sense procedures.

No first aid training? In case of a serious injury, you should make the person as comfortable as possible without risking further injury and call for medical help. In case of a minor injury, give the person whatever aid is necessary from the property's first aid kit, fill out an accident report, and urge the victim to see a physician if that seems appropriate.

First aid training: Encourage employees to receive first aid training throughout the United States. If possible, training should be given to several employees so that it is more likely that someone with first aid training will always be on the premises.

Supplies and information: An operation should have first aid equipment and supplies on site in a convenient area. In large operations, particularly those with more than one floor, several first aid kits may be needed. Display first aid information. Post various types of medical and first aid posters in appropriate places throughout your ghost kitchen operation.

Choking: Choking because of an obstructed airway is a leading cause of accidental death. If a choking person is not coughing or is unable to speak, that's your cue to perform the Heimlich maneuver immediately. The Heimlich maneuver is generally considered the best first aid for choking. However, it is important that you don't carry out the Heimlich maneuver if you haven't received first aid training from a trained professional.

Here are the 10 steps to the Heimlich maneuver: 1) Ask the choking person to stand if he or she is sitting. 2) Place yourself slightly behind the standing person. 3) Reassure the victim that you know the Heimlich maneuver and are going to help. Place your arms around the victim's waist. Make a fist with one hand and place your thumb toward the victim, just above his or her belly button. Grab your fist with your other hand. Deliver five upward squeeze-thrusts into abdomen. Make each squeeze-thrust strong enough to dislodge a foreign body. Understand that your thrusts make the diaphragm move air out of the victim's lungs, creating a kind of artificial cough. Keep a firm grip on the victim, since he or she can lose consciousness and fall to the ground if the Heimlich maneuver is not effective.

Ghost kitchen accident summary: Burns, muscle strains, falls, cuts, equipment accidents, and fire are the most common types of food service accidents in the kitchen. There are numerous ways to reduce the risk of these accidents occurring.

Many burns can be prevented by taking care when using pots and pans. Muscle strains can be prevented by lifting in the correct manner. Keep your back straight and lift with your legs. Risk of falls can be reduced by keeping the floor space clean and tidy, and keeping the work space well-lit.

Some cuts can be prevented by taking extreme care when handling knives. The chances of accidents with equipment can be made less likely by only allowing employees who have been trained in using the equipment to use it, by keeping equipment maintained, and taking care when using it.

The danger of fire can be lessened through properly cleaning and maintaining cooking equipment and exhaust hoods and filters, and using fire detection devices. Having employees with first aid training, if possible, is desired. First aid equipment should be available on the premises. Display first aid information such as appropriate posters throughout the food service operation.

Introduction to water quality: A person responsible for food safety must know the necessary requirements for constructing water systems within the factory. Identifying possible points of contamination or reduction in the quality of the water is essential to maintain the safety of a product. Having poor water quality or using contaminated water in food processing can affect the safety of products and potentially cause illness to many people. A good water quality management system will reduce this risk.

I'll discuss: System development. Importance of water quality. Legal requirements and regulations. Codex requirements. Proper construction of wells and plumbing systems. Monitoring and management.

Learning objectives: Describe reasons for ensuring water quality. Explain the regulations and customer requirements associated with water quality, ice, and steam. Explain the characteristics of properly constructed water wells where applicable and plumbing systems necessary for delivery of potable water, ice, and steam. Design a system to ensure the quality of water, ice, and steam.

System development: As the person responsible for food safety within the ghost kitchen, you must develop systems that ensure that the staff is aware that they must use water during the food production process.

Monitor the staff's use of safe water during the food production process. Ensure that the staff is aware of their responsibility to identify maintenance issues for water systems.

Monitor the staff is aware of hazard prevention practices. Monitor and review the risk analysis used in identifying all possible hazards concerned with water used within the facility.

Any system will have to be clearly and concisely documented and communicated effectively to appropriate staff within the company. You must work closely with key kitchen staff to ensure they clearly understand the importance of such systems and the ways they can influence effective compliance. Since the responsibility for food safety rests with you, direct verification of systems is extremely important for basic level requirements, and you should personally systematically monitor activities on a regular basis and record your findings.

The importance of water quality: The contamination of water can cause serious illnesses to consumers. Water contamination is a major source of gastrointestinal illnesses, which can be fatal to vulnerable people. Pathogenic microorganisms in contaminated water can potentially contaminate foods when used in ingredients, ice, or steam and when there is contact with food.

Chemicals in water can also be a public health concern. It is common in some parts of the world where ground water used in food production may contain arsenic and other compounds which, when consumed by humans, can be very dangerous.

Legal requirements and regulations: Countries or regions typically have legislative requirements for water quality. As the food safety manager, you should refer to the local regulations on using non-potable water in food product processes since they differ from place to place. The World Health Organization has established guidelines for drinking water guidance in the Codex Alimentarius. These may be adopted as a national standard, but such may not always be the case. These regulations are in place to reduce the risk of water contamination and should protect public health if all businesses follow them correctly.

Codex requirements: The Codex provides the following requirements for the use of water in your ghost kitchen facility: Facilities. Water in contact with food. Water as an ingredient. Water used to make ice and steam.

The Codex requirements state that an adequate supply of potable water with appropriate facilities for its storage, distribution, and temperature control should be available whenever necessary to ensure the safety and suitability of food. To find correct guidance for drinking water, you should study the World Health Organization's Guideline for Drinking Water Quality 3. Non-potable water is regularly used in ghost kitchen facilities for fire control, steam production, refrigeration, and other similar purposes where the quality of the water does not matter. Non-potable water must be identified in your facility and must have a separate system from potable systems.

Only potable water should be used if the water is going to be in contact with the food product. There are, however, a few exceptions when this rule does not apply: For steam production. Fire control, and other similar purposes not connected with food in certain food processes. Chilling, and in food handling areas, provided this does not constitute a hazard to the safety and suitability of food; for example, the use of clean seawater.

Water that is recirculated for reuse should be treated and maintained in such a condition that no risk to the safety and suitability of food can result. You must monitor the treatment process effectively to make sure that you have them under control. Water that has been recirculated but has received no further treatment and water that has been recovered from processing of food by evaporation or drying may be used again. This water cannot be used, however, if it poses a risk to the safety and suitability of food.

You must give careful consideration when using water as an ingredient to prevent problems with safety. Potable water must be used wherever necessary to avoid food contamination. A safety problem could occur, for example, when water is used as an ingredient in ice cream. The freezing process does not kill microorganisms, so it is very easy for a person to become ill from eating contaminated ice cream.

Water may also be used as an ingredient in the form of ice or steam. Certain pathogens can survive the ice or steam-making process, thus potentially remaining a risk to health if the ice or steam from this source comes into direct contact with food. Both ice and steam should be produced, handled, and stored to protect them from contaminants.

Many foods have direct contact with steam. The water used in the steaming process should not constitute a threat to the safety and suitability of the products.

Correct construction of wells and plumbing systems: Your kitchen facility must have adequate and safe wells and plumbing systems to prevent risk of contamination by water. As a food safety manager, you should know the requirements for the facility for water usage and also all the systems used. With this knowledge, you can identify any maintenance problems and can thus prevent any subsequent contamination.

The source of potable water to your kitchen facility must be a recognized one, from either a municipal supply or private well. For it to be acceptable for use, the water supply system must be properly constructed, properly maintained, and routinely tested to ensure the safety of the water coming into your ghost kitchen facility. If your facility receives water from a well, the well should be tested at least once a year; however, you should carry out a risk assessment to see how often testing needs to be done. The risk assessment may look at areas such as possible leaking of contaminants from farmland or industrial areas.

You must have potable hot and cold water available in processing areas. There should also be sufficient volume and water pressure to allow appropriate cleaning.

If your kitchen facility has a non-potable water supply which is required to be used as an ingredient or otherwise come into direct contact with food, then this must be effectively purified on site by a number of methods: Sand filtration. Membrane filtration. Charcoal filtration. Reverse osmosis. Ion exchange.

Cross-connection: Any connection or structural arrangement between a potable water system and a non-potable system, liquid or otherwise, through which backflow can occur.

Backflow: The flow of water or other liquids, mixtures, or substances into a potable water system from any source other than the intended source. Backflow, by its very nature of potentially mixing potable and non-potable water systems, can pose a high risk to the consumer's health.

Within any water conveyance system, there are two types of plumbing connections: direct and indirect. Direct connection: A solid physical joining to a waste or soil line. Indirect communication: Other than a solid physical joining to a waste or soil line. It can be either an air gap or an air break.

Air gap: The unobstructed vertical distance through the free atmosphere between the lowest opening from any pipe or outlet supplying fixture, or other device, and the flood level rim of the receptacle. The vertical physical separation must be at least two times the inside diameter of the water inlet pipe above the flood rim level, but cannot be less than one inch.

Air break: A piping arrangement in which a drain from a fixture, appliance, or device discharges indirectly into another fixture, receptacle, or interception at a point below the flood level rim. The connection does not provide an unobstructed vertical distance through the free atmosphere and is not solidly connected but precludes the possibility of backflow to a potable water source into a sink or dishwasher or fixture being drained.

Monitoring and management: The management of water quality in your company is extremely important. You must develop a routine monitoring system to ensure water safety for the various uses in food production. You must also be aware of any risks posed by the design of the water conveyance system; for example, the cross-connections in the plumbing system. When your company commissions any new equipment that uses water, it must be monitored prior to full use to ensure that the safety of water is not compromised.

Now let's touch back up on allergens for your ghost kitchen. Food allergies affect over 15 million Americans and cause hundreds of thousands of hospitalizations every year. Currently, only two states mandate allergy training: Rhode Island and Massachusetts. However, it is important that everyone working in the ghost kitchen food service industry be familiar with food allergies and the special accommodations that should be made for customers with food allergies.

Common food allergies: The "big 8" in food allergies are 8 foods that cause 90% of all allergic reactions. They are: peanuts, milk & dairy, wheat & gluten, shellfish, eggs, fish, soy, tree nuts. Up to 170 additional foods can elicit an allergic response in people.

Symptoms of food allergies: Reactions to food allergies range from mild to severe, but all should be taken seriously. Common reactions include itching or tingling, shortness of breath or wheezing, hives or rash, swelling of the hands or face, abdominal pain or cramps, vomiting and diarrhea, loss of consciousness. Reactions typically occur several minutes to several hours after ingesting the offending food.

Cross-contamination: Cross-contamination occurs when an allergen comes into contact with another type of food. An example would be using a pan to cook shrimp and then using the same oil to cook chicken. There are many ways to prevent cross-contamination from occurring, but here is a short list: Ensure food is always properly labeled so you know what is in it. Always properly clean cookware, servingware, cutting boards, and utensils after each use. Wash hands before and after handling of different types of foods. Store meats in well-sealed containers and on a low level to prevent the juice from contaminating other types of food underneath.

Related foods: Certain allergy-producing foods may be referred to by different names depending on their state. For example, whey is the liquid that remains after milk has been curdled or strained and is a common ingredient in many products. Lecithin is a highly processed food related to soy. Being familiar with foods that contain common allergens is also important. For example, chocolate and butter contain milk, so they may pose a problem for those with a milk allergy.

Now, let's dive into more about ServSafe and safety exam. About the job: An employee in the food service may be involved in the cooking process or participate in various other capacities, including preparing cold food and serving beverages. According to the National Occupational Research Agenda, there are presently over 9 million food service employees in the United States. However, with ghost kitchens, that number is increasing.

The food service business ranges from newly ghost kitchens, food trucks, full-service restaurants, to schools and health facilities, such as nursing homes. Each year, a large number of young people get their first job as a food service. Employers require their food and alcohol service workers to have ServSafe certification.

Salary: Bureau of Labor Statistics data shows that the average hourly wage for a food service employee is $9.35/hour, but that this can reach nearly $16.00/hour for certain positions. Some food service positions also include a significant income from customer tips, which is only limited by the employee's dedication to good service.

About the test: ServSafe is a group of 3 individual multiple-choice tests, each of which can lead to certification in a specific part of the food service industry. There are tests for food service handling, food service manager, and responsible alcohol service, primary and advanced. A fourth test, ServSafe

Allergens, is currently only required in Massachusetts and Rhode Island, though will likely be picked up by other states in the near future.

The ServSafe program is administered by the National Restaurant Association, which makes training and testing materials available. ServSafe certification is accepted nationwide in the United States. The test is available in a number of languages, besides English, and is given in either paper or computer versions.

While coursework and testing can both be done online, certain tests require a proctor, which means even the online versions must be completed in a testing center. ServSafe is the name for several food service certification exams. The 3 main types are listed here. ServSafe also has some state-specific courses and exams available, such as the Texas Food Guard.

Costs for the online course and exam are listed as: Food Handlers $15.00, Manager $125.00, Alcohol Safety $30.00, Allergens $22.00. Certificates and retests have additional costs. There may be different fees for locally offered courses and exams.

Availability: Both ServSafe coursework and exams are available in person and online. You are allowed to choose either option for the two parts of this process in any combination. Note that online exams for the Food Handler and Alcohol/Primary do not require a proctor. All other exams, whether print or online, do require a proctor and would need to be taken at a test center.

To find an instructor/proctor in your area, check out the ServSafe website. Retesting: You may retest once with no waiting period. After that, you must wait 60 days before retesting a second time. During one year, you may take the same ServSafe test up to 4 times.

Eligibility: The ServSafe courses and exams have no prerequisite, although course completion may be required for exams in some jurisdictions. Course completion is required for access to the online exam. An online or in-person training program may be required by a state or locality before a local exam. Check your local and state requirements for ServSafe exams on the ServSafe website.

Why it matters: Passing a ServSafe exam may determine your ability to be hired in a food or alcohol service capacity. Additional certification in managing food and/or alcohol service may then enable you to acquire advanced positions within the company. Certification in several areas can certainly expand your employment possibilities in the food service field. Once you acquire any ServSafe certification, it will be good for 5 years.

Let's move forward to ServSafe manager. Food safety and contamination: Many food safety and contamination concerns are matters of common sense. Food should be both heated and cooled to certain temperatures, should not be left out for extended periods of time, should be covered and stored properly, should be stored separately from chemicals and cleaners, etc.

Following these guidelines will not only ensure that food is kept safe from foodborne illnesses and contaminants, that it is imbued with the highest quality and care possible.

Foodborne illnesses: Foodborne illnesses are illnesses bred from bacterial food contamination. These include illnesses such as E. Coli and Listeriosis, infection from Listeria exposure. Ensuring foods remain free from foodborne illnesses can be achieved in 2 ways: through proper storage and proper cooking.

Proper storage requires that food handlers store all food in temperatures below 41° Fahrenheit for refrigeration, and exceeding 135° Fahrenheit storing hot and cooking. Foods held between these temperatures should only be given a 4-hour window before they are either placed back into storage or thrown away.

Foods being cooked should first be cooked to 135° Fahrenheit and higher to kill any remaining germs. While the majority of foodborne illnesses result from bacterial contamination, some illnesses have been caused by viruses and diseases from food service workers. For this reason, it is vitally important to wear protective gear when handling food, keeping hair away from food and avoiding skin-to-food contact, and the practice proper hygiene, through washing your hands for a minimum of 20-30 seconds with hot water and soap.

While foodborne illnesses pose a risk to everyone, certain populations are more at risk than others. They are the elderly, younger children, and people who are immunocompromised.

Biological, physical, and chemical contaminants: Food contamination takes on many different forms, including biological, physical ,and chemical forces, as well as potential allergens. Contamination can occur due to improper food storage, storing food next to chemicals, to improper growing conditions, to exposure to parasites, and to the incorrect use of preparation materials.

Biological contaminants: Biological contaminants are contaminants found in nature. These include bacteria, parasites, fungi, and environmental toxins. The best way to prevent contamination from biological agents is to adhere to food storage and preparation guidelines, keeping foods at the proper temperatures during storage and cooking.

Bacteria thrives in moist environments between 41° Fahrenheit. The FDA considers 3 types of bacteria as most dangerous because they are very contagious and cause severe illnesses: Salmonella Typhi, Shigella, and Escherichia Coli, more commonly referred to as E. Coli.

Salmonella comes from people and is often found in beverages or ready-to-eat foods such as fruits and vegetables. The best way to prevent salmonella is to wash your hands and ensure all food is cooked to the proper temperature.

Shigella originates from human feces. It is spread from flies and improper hand-washing. The best way to prevent shigella is to observe good hygiene practices and eliminate insects around food.

E. Coli originates from cattle intestines, and is found in ground beef or fresh produce that may be contaminated from farm runoff, such as lettuce or strawberries. The best way to avoid E. Coli is to avoid cross-contamination between ground beef and other foods and to always wash produce before ingestion.

Viruses don't grow in food but can be transferred to food through the fecal-oral route. Sneezing, coughing, and improper hand-washing practices are some of the most common routes of transmission. Hepatitis A and the Norovirus are the most common viruses found in food. They are typically linked in with ready-to-eat foods and shellfish.

Parasites are most often found in seafood, wild game meats, and food that has been washed with contaminated water. To eliminate parasites, always cook foods to the recommended temperature. If the seafood or meat is supposed to be served undercooked or raw, such as sushi or sashimi, ensure it is stored at the proper temperature and served to the guest immediately.

Fungi includes yeasts, molds, and mushrooms. Fungi pose a problem when they produce toxins that can make the consumer sick. Always be sure the mushrooms you are serving are safe to eat, and throw out any food that has developed mold. In addition to the typical vomiting/diarrhea that many foodborne illnesses cause, ingesting toxic fungi can also cause neurological symptoms, such as a reverse hot/cold sensation or tingling in the extremities.

Physical contaminants refer to contaminants of an actual foreign physical object. These can include insects or other foreign pests in food or may refer to shards of broken metal or other small, potentially hazardous objects that may be found in food. This also includes human items such as fingernails, hair, and skin.

The best means of avoiding this particular contaminant is through a thorough inspection of food items and observation of safe food preparation and hygiene guidelines.

Chemical contaminants are contaminants from cleaning supplies, improper surface materials, improper metals, and pesticides. While some pesticide exposure cannot be avoided in conventional foods, thorough cleaning of pesticide-exposed food greatly lessens the chemical contaminant.

To avoid chemical contaminant in other mediums, store and use cleaning materials a great distance from all food items, and wait the recommended time before using a surface cleaned with chemical agents. Adhere to the rules of food preparation and avoid using soft or unsafe metals and plastics in cooking.

Allergens: While allergens are not unsafe for everyone, even the slightest amount of exposure to food allergy can prove toxic. For this reason, you must acquaint yourself with the equipment you use, the manufacturing facilities your food employs, and the ingredients found in your food items.

To avoid allergen exposure during food preparation, be sure to clean and sanitize surfaces and utensils before and after each use. Acquaint yourself with common food allergies, and be aware of the presence of these allergens in your food, especially if your ghost kitchen has take-out and dining-in. Common allergies again include nuts, dairy, soy, gluten, fish, and wheat.

The flow of food: As food comes in-and-out of your ghost kitchen establishment, it requires safe handling and preparation. While it may seem simple enough to receive and store food, you must ensure that all received food is stored properly and is within its safe use dates. As food enters and leaves an establishment, it must constantly be monitored for freshness and safety.

Purchasing, receiving, and storing: When purchasing food, always be sure to purchase from reputable establishments. While it may be tempting to your ghost kitchen to ship food in from unapproved areas and vendors, or to go for the cheapest food option and outsourcing, adhering to safety guidelines while producing and storing food is pivotal. Read company statements and practices before deciding to purchase with that particular entity, and make sure safe practices are being followed.

When food is being received, it must adhere to all federal and state guidelines. In addition, you must ensure that all food is delivered at safe temperatures. Here are some more bonus tip guidelines to keep in mind. 41° or colder for cold foods. 45° or lower for live shellfish, milk, and eggs.

All frozen foods must remain frozen during delivery. No matter which type of food you are handling, it should always be promptly stored after being received. Proper food storage has been touched on, be can be restated here: cold foods should be stored at 41° Fahrenheit or lower, while hot foods must be stored at 135° Fahrenheit or higher. Failure to do so will result in the introduction of foodborne illness due to bacterial contamination.

Preparation: As mentioned above, proper food preparation is essential in delivering safe, high-quality food. When cooking, vegetables and fruits should be cooked to 135°

Fahrenheit or higher, while meats should be cooked to 165 degrees Fahrenheit or higher.

Before cooking, food should be thawed via cool water, a refrigerator, or a microwave.

Serving: When serving food, be keenly aware of all food temperatures. Food should not be allowed to remain between 41° Fahrenheit for more than 4 hours; food left out for more than 4 hours must be discarded.

Serving already-served food is not permitted unless food is sealed and untouched. Finally, self-service stations should only be used with fresh plates. Patrons/staff should not be permitted to reuse dirty plates or utensils because this can contaminate dishes placed out for service.

Let's move forward into food safety management systems. Before ghost kitchen employees are permitted to work with food, safety programs should have taken place instructing the proper implementation of personal hygiene, food service and preparation, and managerial practices. Managerial practices include constantly checking food stations and workers to ensure the necessary practices are being observed. Management should also never admit fault in the case of a foodborne illness outbreak. Instead management should work to discover the initial culprit and immediately eradicate said cause.

Cleaning and sanitation are extremely important in maintaining a well-rounded, safe eating environment. Proper cleaning will help eradicate pests such as mice and cockroaches, while sanitation will assist in warding off foodborne illness and cross-contamination between food items. Following the procedures for cleaning and sanitizing will ensure both workers and customers enjoy a hassle-free, safe dining or take-out delivery experience.

Principles of cleaning and sanitation: Cleaning and sanitizing are different actions but generally go hand-in-hand. Cleaning is the process of removing food or other items from surface; sanitizing is the act of removing organisms from a surface to improve safety and reduce the risk of exposure to harmful bacteria or fungi. The two come together in compound process: wash, rinse, sanitize, and air dry.

Failure to complete these steps in that order will result in an ineffective washing and sanitizing process. Both cleaning and sanitizing agents should be stored well away from food items, and rags and other cleaning tools should be changed at least every 4 hours to prevent contamination.

Pest management involves 3 steps: 1) Deny pests access to the establishment. 2) Deny pests food, water, and shelter. 3) Work with a licensed pets control operator to remove any pests that have made a home for themselves.

While pest prevention is best, be on the lookout for signs of any existing pest issues. These include roach droppings and egg casings, pepper-like spots and cases that look like thick grains of dark rice, and rodent droppings and actions including gnawing, nesting, and leaving tracks. Just as cleaning agents should be stored away from food, on-site pest removal agents must be stored away from food. Professional pest removal should be completed after business hours and after employees have gone home, and all surfaces should be cleaned and sanitized thoroughly before use.

Now, let's take a deep dive in depth into control of food hazards. Overview: You need comprehensive knowledge to control food hazards within your ghost kitchen. Lack of the control of hazards can cause contamination, resulting in risks to consumer health or loss of product, leading to significant financial loss. Food hazards can be biological, chemical, or physical in nature. As a food safety manager, you should be aware of the significance of hazards and must be able to identify and monitor hazards within your production process. This overview layout covers the requirements for effective general and specific controls to prevent food hazards. I will review the following topics with a final discussion: System development, biological hazards, chemical hazards, physical hazards, control of food safety hazards.

Learning objectives: Describe the principles and reasons for controlling food hazards. Explain the nature of food safety hazards—biological, chemical, physical, and allergens—and factors influencing the likelihood of their occurrence, such as conditions that influence food safety hazards commonly associated with specific foods produced as well as customer requirements and legislation.

Explain the recognized and known control measures and how to apply these to control hazards relevant to specific products, taking into consideration local regulatory compliance and customer requirements. Design the monitoring procedures necessary to ensure control of food safety hazards relevant to the product. Perform corrective actions when control measures are not achieved. Operate a system for maintaining comprehensive records in relation to the control of identified hazards.

System development: As the person responsible for food safety within the kitchen facility, it is important to develop a system to ensure and monitor that the staff is fully aware of and uses: Good biological hazard prevention practices. Good physical hazard prevention practices. Risk analysis processes to identify all possible hazards.

Any system will have to be clearly and concisely documented and communicated effectively to appropriate staff within the kitchen. It is important to work closely with key kitchen staff to ensure that they clearly understand the importance of such systems and the ways they can influence effective ghost kitchen compliance. Since the responsibility for food safety rests with you, direct verification of systems is extremely important for basic level requirements. You should personally monitor activities on a regular basis and record your findings.

Food safety: When considering food safety, you must understand the difference between quality and safety.

Food Safety Codex Standards assures that food will not cause harm when prepared and/or eaten according to its intended use. Food safety refers to attributes that cannot be directly observed, but instead require laboratory procedures for their measurement. These procedures include microbiological techniques or chemical analysis.

Food quality: Refers to attributes that can be readily observed by sight, smell, or simple measurement such as color or condition. Food quality is easier to assess than food safety.

Food Safety Hazard Codex Standards: A biological, chemical or physical agent in, or condition of, food with the potential to cause an adverse health effect. Food safety hazards include bacteria, viruses, parasites, hazardous chemicals, and foreign materials that can cause an adverse health effect to a consumer.

In food safety management systems, hazards refer to conditions or contaminants in foods that can cause illness or injury. It is important to understand that hazards do not refer to undesirable conditions or contaminants such as presence of insects, spoilage, hair or dirt, violations of regulatory food standards not directly related to safety.

Biological hazards: There are a number of different types of biological hazards that can be present within food. These are typically microorganisms and include bacteria, viruses, and parasites. Control points for biological hazards must be identified during the process and storage of food products. This can be done by using hazards analysis techniques.

Microorganisms are small, living unicellular or multicellular organisms. They include bacteria, viruses, yeasts, molds, and parasites. These are not all necessarily bad for humans; in fact, many can be beneficial to humans. There are different types of microorganisms: helpful, spoilage, and disease-causing–pathogenic.

Helpful microorganisms can be added to foods or are found naturally in them. In many cases, microorganisms are used in foods to help with preservation but can also be added to create unique flavors and textures. Food such as sauerkraut and pickles utilize fermentation as a preservation process and use microorganisms to carry out this fermentation process. Other foods such as bread use fermentation as an essential part of their production.

Spoilage microorganisms affect the quality of the product, not necessarily the safety of the food. It is usually very easy to identify when a food product is affected by spoilage, by look or taste. There can be discoloration on fruits, molds on bread, or milk that tastes sour. In some cases spoilage microorganisms can affect the safety of products.

An example is that some fruits can decay by a mold called penicillium expansum. This mold produces a toxin that can affect humans. Any food found to be spoilt should be disposed of immediately, and products in the same lot should be inspected.

Disease-causing, pathogenic microorganisms can cause illnesses that can range from mild to life-threatening. These microorganisms are the most serious, so you must develop procedures to eliminate the risk of their contaminating products.

Examples of these microorganisms that should be effectively controlled are bacteria such as salmonella or E. Coli 0157:H7. The common symptoms of these are nausea, vomiting and diarrhea, and, in serious cases, death.

Pathogens are microorganisms that cause foodborne illness. Pathogens come in 3 forms: bacteria, single-celled organisms that live independently, and viruses, small particles that live and replicate in a host. Parasites. Intestinal worms or protozoa that live in a host animal or human.

Pathogens can be found in soils; these include: Salmonella species. E. Coli 0157:H7. Shigella species. Campylobacter jejuni. Viruses and parasites. The presence of these pathogens within humans is the main reason why washing your hands after using the toilet is essential in your ghost kitchen when working with any food.

Bacteria are very resilient microorganisms that are found everywhere. Some examples of where they can live and multiply are: air, soil, and water. In intestines of animals and humans. On skins of fruit and vegetables. On raw meat, poultry, and seafood. On shells or nuts. On insects and rodents. On hands, skin, hair, and clothing of people.

Biological hazards: Because of the nature and diversity of bacteria, they can be found almost anywhere in your kitchen facility. It is, therefore, imperative that bacteria and other microorganisms are controlled to acceptable levels and, in some cases, completely eliminated in the food. The problem of bacteria when concerned with food safety is that they are single-celled organisms that can live independently. When the conditions are correct, they can divide and multiply very quickly. To multiply, bacteria need moisture, nutrients, warmth, and time. Moisture and nutrients are found on most foods, so bacterial growth on foods is very common.

Bacteria cause the greatest number of deaths from foodborne illness. They are impossible to see with the naked eye. Taking these factors into account, it is clear that controlling bacteria can be difficult but is essential.

Viruses are different from bacteria since they don't multiply in food. They are intracellular organisms that invade living cells and then use the cell's content to replicate. Since viruses don't multiply on food, they contaminate by human or animal interaction. Foodborne viral diseases generally result from poor personal hygiene or lack of pest control. Viruses can also survive and travel in water and ice, so it is essential that your water supply is adequate, safe, and regularly monitored.

Personal hygiene for food handlers is extremely important in controlling viruses. All staff must be made aware of inappropriate personal hygiene practices, and monitoring should take place to ensure good personal hygiene is being followed in your ghost kitchen. Staff members who show symptoms of viral infection should be identified and kept away from food-processing areas.

If a food handler has a viral infection, then it is very easy to spread that virus. It is good practice to have a return-to-work policy in place for staff who have been absent as a result of viral infection, allowing you thus to identify any viral symptoms that may still be present. Viruses can be transmitted in water; potable water must, therefore, be used for ice-making or as an ingredient in food.

Parasites can be unicellular or multicellular microorganisms. They can colonize in the gastrointestinal tract of humans and other animals. More often than not these parasites have really complex life cycles where they may be in a human's intestinal tract for a long period of time and shed cysts. These cysts are a protected form of themselves and can infect other people or animals when they are consumed. The most common foodborne parasites are protozoan parasites and parasitic worms.

Protozoan parasites, which are unicellular organisms, are the most common foodborne or waterborne parasites. They are so common in some parts of the world that they are endemic. Examples of protozoan parasites include: Giardia lamblia. Cryptosporidium parvum. Cyclospora cayetanesis. Toxoplasma gondii.

Parasitic worms are small, multicellular organisms that can colonize in the gastrointestinal tract or other tissues of humans or animals. Some common parasitic worms include: Anasakis simplex and related worms. Other seafood-associated parasitic worms. Trichinella spiralis and related Trichinella species. Ascaris lumbricoides. Trichuris trichiura.

Since parasites can be found in feces, there is a risk of contamination when using manure for fruit and vegetable crops. Consider using compost that does not contain manure to remove the risk of this parasitic contamination. Since parasites can live in water, you must use potable water for washing, packing, and processing food products. Thermal processing can destroy parasites; so if appropriate, use this treatment to remove the parasite risk.

Product specification: It is important to be aware of the presence and number of microorganisms in food. Many raw materials, therefore, have microbiological standards. It is common in the food industry to have specifications for the absence of microbiological contaminants.

Control mechanisms: Physical and chemical control mechanisms significantly affect the survival and multiplication of microorganisms; for example, a reduction in pH in fruit juice by the addition of ascorbic acid can prevent microorganisms from multiplying. Time and temperature are important control points since cooking or freezing rapidly can prevent the growth of biological contaminants. Freezing usually stops the multiplication of microorganisms; however, it does not kill them. Thermal processing will kill most biological hazards.

Cross-contamination: Cross-contamination must be managed so that materials cannot contaminate others. Control systems should be in place and your kitchen staff made aware of their responsibility to prevent contamination. Your staff must also be aware of correct product handling and personal hygiene.

Cleaning and disinfection: The equipment used for producing, processing, and storing products should be sanitized on a regular basis. It is good practice to have a cleaning schedule in place. The packing, storage, and distribution must be controlled so that no biological hazard can contaminate or survive on food products. This process will entail suitable packaging for the product and temperature control in storage and distribution.

Conditions for use: The directions you provide to the consumer are very important. Providing information on how to correctly store and cook the product can reduce the risk of biological hazards.

Chemical hazards: There are different types of chemical hazards associated with food: Naturally-occurring chemicals.

Intentionally-added chemicals. Unintentional or incidental chemical additives.

Control points for chemical hazards must be identified during the process and storage of food products. Such can be done using hazard analysis technique.

There is a perception that if something is naturally grown or raised, it will not have any chemical hazards present. This belief is not true; naturally-occurring chemical hazards are present in many foods. For example, there are toxins found in many varieties of mushrooms and some seafood. In many countries there is legislation relating to the presence or level of toxins, so you should be aware using foods that may contain these toxins. It would be good practice to refer to legislation and analysis samples of the product before use. These chemical hazards are often classified as biological, but the important thing is that it be recognized as a hazard and controlled.

Examples of naturally-occurring chemical hazards are: Toxins are produced by Clostridium botulinum, Staphylococcus aureus, Bacillus cereus, scombrotoxin (histamine)–fish, Saxitoxin-paralytic shellfish toxin, Ciguatoxin–fish, Mycotoxins produced by molds (fungi).

There are 2 types of intentionally added chemicals: direct and indirect food additives. Direct Additives: Direct additives are compounds such as preservatives; these include nitrites, sodium benzoate, and sulfiting agents. You must be aware of the regulations relating to the use of these compounds since legislation does differ from country to country. Additives such as colors and nutritional additives such as vitamins are also direct. All direct additives must be included on all labels.

Indirect Additives: Indirect food additives include adhesives, paper and paperboard components, polymers, adjuvants, protection aids, and sanitizers. In most cases these indirect food additives are undesirable and migrate into the food from inappropriate packaging.

There are a number of unintentionally introduced chemicals added to foods by agricultural processing, including pesticides, fungicides, herbicides, fertilizers, antibiotics, growth hormones.

These substances are prohibited in certain countries. To ensure your company is complying with legislation where the food is sold, you should carefully review the appropriate legislation. There are private standards and business-to-business requirements that can be stricter than legislative requirements, and the customer will closely scrutinize the product for the presence and level of substances that violate these standards.

Having a management system in place that identifies sampling points and sampling levels is good practice to reduce the risk of chemical hazards.

Physical hazards: A physical hazard is any potential harmful extraneous matter not normally found in food. They are different to biological or chemical hazards; they generally cause problems for relatively few consumers per incident. The result of personal injuries is usually not life-threatening but can cause considerable personal distress to the consumer. Typical examples are broken teeth, cut mouths, and choking.

Examples of physical hazards is metal fragments, glass particles, wood splinters, rock fragments, stones, bone fragments in meat and poultry.

Control points for physical hazards must be identified during the process and storage of food products. Such can be done by using a hazard analysis technique.

Preventive maintenance of equipment is extremely important to greatly reduce the risk of physical contamination.

Equipment failure or breakage can allow physical hazards to enter foods. This happens usually during the processing stage. Routine inspections and maintenance of the equipment is good practice. Screens and filters used in liquid processing can identify problems in equipment upstream. By regularly inspecting the screens or filters, objects from equipment like broken machine parts or rubber seals, for example, can easily be seen and further contamination reduced.

Detection equipment is very useful in identifying physical hazards in foods. There are a number of methods that can be used for different processes: Magnet—ferrous metal. Metal detector—ferrous and non-ferrous metals. X-ray equipment all types of physical hazards. Screen or sifter—separation by size. Aspirator—segregation by weight. Bone separator—mechanically separated meat.

The staff can pose a risk to foods by physical hazard contamination. In order to prevent/reduce this risk, your staff must be made aware of company policies in regard to hazard prevention. An example is the wearing of jewelry. Your staff should also be encouraged to make you aware of any risk of possible physical product contamination they observe while at work. As a food safety manager, you must have in place an effective management system that identifies the source and control points to reduce the risk of physical hazards.

Control of food safety hazards: To control food safety hazards effectively, it is important to understand the nature of possible hazards. Not all substances or microorganisms are hazardous until they reach a certain level, so it is important to know and understand the significance of these levels. Possible hazards are always going to pose a risk to your company, so it is essential to know how to control these hazards. By using different methods such as destroying, removing, preventing, or reducing hazards to an acceptable level, contamination issues will be greatly reduced.

To control food hazards, you must have a system in place that maintains control points within the process. You must have knowledge of how to develop this system so that any change can be taken into account and managed correctly.

Now, let's address another one of the most vital aspects for your ghost kitchen finally with kitchen equipment, and tools built for your menu and cooking stations. Choosing the right equipment fit or suitable for your style of foods and differences you're cooking. From fryers, grills, and griddles. Grinding, slicing, mixing, and pureeing. To refrigeration (coolers or freezers), ranges and ovens. Also the right usage of tools and equipment. Streamline the process with proper equipment and tools for your ghost kitchen and menu dishes. Streamline is to make simpler or more efficient, put in order or bring up to date.

If you choose to have a deep fryer, this consists of a gas or electric heating element and a large stainless-steel reservoir that holds the fat. A thermostat allows the user to control the temperature of the fat. Stainless-steel wire mesh baskets are used to lower and lift foods into and out of the fat.

Grills and griddles: Griddles are similar to a flattop range; a griddle has a heat source located beneath a thick plate of metal, generally cast iron or steel. The food is cooked directly on the griddle surface.

Grill/Broiler/Salamander: In a grill, the heat source is located below a rack; in a broiler or salamander, the heat source is above. Some units have adjustable racks that allow the food to be raised or lowered to control cooking speed. Some grills burn wood, charcoal, or both, but units in ghost kitchens are often either gas or electric fired, with ceramic "rocks" that create a bed of coals to produce the effect of a charcoal grill. Broilers radiate an intense heat from above and can be found as a setting in a gas or electric oven. If the broiler is contained as a separate unit, it is known as a salamander and is used primarily to finish or glaze foods. You can Google all 3 and see the different options for your ghost kitchen based on what you're cooking and the quantity. Remember for better and timely results, the more all your kitchen equipment is going to cost usually.

With a broiler and salamander equipment, the heat source is located above the rack. A stainless steel basket is used to lower and lift foods into and out of fat in a deep fryer. When a broiler is contained as a separate unit, it is known as a salamander. The thickness of the heat plate makes a griddle maintain its heat better. A fat vac is used to transport old oil to be disposed. A thermostat helps maintain proper heat in a griddle. Volume of fat, temperature recovery, number of burners all are some important considerations when looking for a deep fryer. The number of burners and depth of a grill is responsible for how well the unit operates. Some deep fryers are programmatically controlled. Food is cooked directly on the griddle's surface.

I wanted to leave you some more bonus tips to add value to your ghost kitchen in your equipment selection/hunting process. Let's further dive into other equipment you may need or select for your ghost kitchen.

Ranges and ovens: Ranges types. The stovetop is known as the range; the oven is usually below the range. However, there are a number of variations on this standard arrangement. Gas or electric ranges are available in many sizes and with different combinations of open burners, flattops (not to be confused with griddle units), and ring tops. Open burners and ring tops supply direct heat, which is easy to change and control. Flattops provide indirect heat, which is more even and less intense than direct heat.

Foods that require long, slow cooking, such as stocks, are more effectively cooked on a flattop. Small units known as candy stoves or stockpot ranges have rings of gas jets or removable rings under a flattop, allowing for excellent heat control. Ovens cook foods by surrounding them with hot air, a gentler and more even source of heat than the direct heat of a burner.

Open-burner range: This type range has individual grate-style burners that allow for easy adjustment of heat. Flattop range: This consists of a thick plate of cast iron or steel set over the heat source. Flattops give relatively even and consistent heat but do not allow for quick adjustment of temperature. Ring-top range: This is a flattop with plates that can be removed to widen the opening, supplying more or less heat. Induction cooktop: This relies on the magnetic attraction between the cooktop and steel or cast iron in the pan to generate heat. The cooktop itself remains cool. Reaction time is significantly faster than for traditional burners. Pans containing copper or aluminum may not be used. You can also Google these as well for your selection.

Ovens: Convection oven. Fans force hot air to circulate around the food, cooking it evenly and quickly. Some convection ovens have the capacity to introduce moisture.

Conventional/deck oven: The heat source is located on the bottom, underneath the deck floor of the oven. Heat is conducted through the deck to the cavity. Conventional ovens can be located below a range top or as separate shelves arranged one above another. The latter are known as deck ovens, and the food is placed directly on the deck instead of on a wire rack. Deck ovens normally consist of 2 to 4 decks, although single-deck models are available.

Combination oven: This piece of equipment, powered by either gas or electricity, is a combination steamer and convection oven. It can be used in steam mode, hot-air convection mode, or heat/steam (combi) mode.

Microwave oven: This oven used electricity to generate microwave radiation, which cooks or reheats foods very quickly. Some models double as convection ovens.

Moving on to hand tools. All these following small hand tools are available to chefs and cooks in your ghost kitchen, and could be part of your knife kit: Palette knife, offset spatula, whisk, peelers, rolling pin, pastry bag, and Parisienne scoop (melon baller).

Rotary or swivel-bladed peeler. Blade may be mounted horizontally or vertically on the handle. Blade is typically 2-3 inches long. Peeling skin from vegetables and fruits. Swivel action accommodates contours of ingredients.

Parisienne scoop (melon baller). May have one scoop or two of different sizes, between ¼ and ¾ inch diameter. Scooping out balls or ovals from vegetables and fruits.

Kitchen fork. A fork with two long tines approximately 4-6 inches long. Testing doneness of braised meats and vegetables; lifting finished items to the carving board or plate; holding an item being carved in place.

Palette knife/metal spatula. Flexible round-tipped tool, may be flat or offset. Blade is between 4 and 5 inches long and ½-¾ inch wide. In the kitchen and bake shop, spreading fillings and glazes; placing garnishes; portioning; and a variety of other functions.

Whisks. Balloon whisks are sphere-shaped and have thin wires to incorporate air when making foams. Sauce whisks are narrower and frequently have thicker wires. Beating, blending, and whipping.

Offset spatula. Blade is chisel-edged, between 9-10 inches long and 3-4 inches wide, set in a short handle. Turning or lifting foods on grills, broilers, and griddles.

Rolling pins. Two types: French-style long cylinder of wood rolled over with palm of hands and rod-and-bearing pin heavier and wider. Rolling out dough.

Pastry bag. Made of plastic, canvas or nylon. Pipe out pureed foods, whipped cream and various toppings.

Small equipment. Measuring equipment. Measuring spoons. Thermometers. Food scales. Digital scales. Graduated measuring pitchers.

Measuring tools. Graduated measuring pitchers. Available in pint, quart and gallon sizes. Measuring liquids. Scales. Spring type, balance beams or electronic scales available in ounce/gram and pound/kilo. Weigh ingredients for preparation and portion control. Thermometers. Available in instant-read, candy and deep-fat thermometers. Measures food's internal temperature. Measuring spoons. Come in tablespoons, half-teaspoon and quarter-teaspoon sizes. Measure small amounts of ingredients.

Sieves and strainers. Sieves and strainers are used to sift, aerate, and help remove any large impurities from dry ingredients. They are also used to drain or puree cooked or raw foods. The delicate mesh of some strainers is highly vulnerable to damage; never drop these into a pot sink, where they could be crushed or torn.

Let's go over a colander, food mill, drum sieve, cheesecloth, conical sieve. Food mill. A flat, curving blade is rotated over a disk by a hand-operated crank. Most professional models have interchangeable disks with holes of varying fineness. Used to puree soft foods. Drum sieve (tamis). Consist of a tinned-steel, nylon, or stainless-steel screen stretched in aluminum or wood frame. Sifting or pureeing.

Conical sieve (chinois). Has openings in the cone that can vary in size from very large to very small. Straining and/or pureeing food. Colander. Available in a variety of sizes, is a stainless-steel or aluminum sieve, with or without a base. Used to strain or drain foods. Ricer. Pierced hopper in which cooked food, often potatoes, is placed. A plate on the end of a lever pushes the food through the holes in the hopper. Make cooked food into small pieces. Cheesecloth. Light, fine-mesh cotton gauze. Used with or in place of a fine conical sieve. Essential for straining some sauces.

Mixing bowls and storage containers. Large storage containers, mixing bowls, and small storage containers. Bowls for mixing. Most kitchens are equipped with a variety of bowls, usually made of a nonreactive material such as stainless steel. Copper bowls are often included in the kitchen's stock of mixing bowls, because they are considered best for whipping egg whites. Bowls should be reserved for mixing, if at all possible, rather than being used for storage.

Storage containers. Foods in the kitchen may be stored raw, partially prepared, or cooked. It is crucial to have an adequate stock of containers to hold foods safely in the refrigerator or freezer. In addition to plastic or stainless-steel containers with or without fitted lids, you will require butcher's paper, plastic wrap, foil and freezer wrap. Tools for securing and marking stored foods include freezer or masking tape and waterproof markers.

Pots, pans and molds. Pots and pans used on the stovetop may be made from a variety of materials, but they must be able to withstand direct heat from a flame. A poorly produced pot will have weak spots and will warp. Pans may be made of many different materials, and selection in large part weighs on preference. Heat conductivity and evenness of heat transfer are important to consider as well as the maintenance of the pan; for example, copper is great for conductivity but requires significant time and labor for proper upkeep. Nonstick coatings may be useful for some applications, but these surfaces are not as sturdy as metal, so another choice for nonstick cookery would be cast iron. Blue-steel and black-steel, pressed-steel, or rolled-steel pans are often preferred to sauteing because of their quick response to changes in temperature.

When choosing a pot or pan, consider the following information: 1) Choose a size appropriate to the food being cooked. Be familiar with the capacity of various pots, pans, and molds. If too many pieces of meat are crowded into a sauteuse, for instance, the food will not brown properly. If the sauteuse is too large, however, the food (Maillard drippings from the meat) could scorch. If a small fish is poached in a large pot, the cuisson (cooking liquid) will not have the proper intensity of flavor.

2) Choose material appropriate to the cooking technique. Experience has shown, and science has verified, that certain cooking techniques are more successful when used with certain materials. For instance, sauteed foods require pans that transmit heat quickly and are sensitive to temperature changes. Braises, on the other hand, require long, fairly gentle cooking; it is more important that the pot transmit heat evenly and hold it well than respond rapidly to changes in heat.

3) Use proper handling, cleaning, and storing techniques. Avoid subjecting pots to heat extremes and rapid changes in temperature (e.g., placing a smoking-hot pot into a sinkful of water) because some materials are prone to warping. Other materials may chip or even crack if allowed to sit over heat when they are empty or if they are handled roughly. Casseroles or molds made of enameled cast iron or steel are especially vulnerable.

Most common stovetops pots and pans. Stockpot/marmite. Large pot, taller than it is wide, with straight sides; may have a spigot. Saucepan. Has straight or slightly flared sides and a single long handle. Sauce pot. Similar to a stockpot in shape, although not as large; has straight sides and two loop handles. Rondeau. Wide, fairly shallow pot with two loop handles. When made from cast iron, frequently known as a "griswold"; may have a single short handle rather than two loop handles. A brasier is similar; may be square instead of round. Sauteuse/saute pan. Shallow skillet with sloping sides and a single long handle. Sautoir/fry pan. Shallow skillet with straight sides and a single long handle. Omelet pan/crepe pan. Shallow skillet with very short, slightly sloping sides; most often made of rolled or blue steel. Bain-marie/double boiler. Nesting pots with single long handle. "Bain-marie" also refers to stainless-steel containers used to hold food in a steam table. Griddle. Flat with no sides; may be built directly into stove. Fish poacher. Long, narrow lidded pot with straight sides; includes a perforated rack for holding fish. Steamer. Pair of stacked pots; lidded top pot has a perforated bottom. Also, bamboo basket with tight-fitting lid; can sit in a wok. Specialty pots and pans. Woks, couscousieres, paella pans and grill pans are used to prepare special, usually ethnic dishes.

Pans for oven cooking. Pans used in ovens are produced from the same basic materials used to make stovetop pots and pans. Glazed and unglazed earthenware, glass, and ceramics are also used. The heat of the oven is less intense than that of a burner, making it possible to use these more delicate materials without risk of cracking or shattering. Metal pans are available in several gauges (gauges refers to the thickness of the metal). Heavy-gauge pans are usually preferred because they transfer heat more evenly. Regarding heat conductivity, some metals heat faster than others.

Aluminum heats quickly but is susceptible to burning food if it is a light gauge. On the other hand, stainless steel is a poor conductor of heat, while materials such as glass, ceramic, and earthenware hold heat well but transfer it poorly.

Oven pans and molds. Roasting pan. Rectangular pan with medium-high sides; comes in various sizes. Roasting or baking. Sheet pan. Very shallow rectangular pan; may be full or half size. Baking storage. Hotel pan/steam. Table pan/chafing dish. Rectangular pans, available in a wide range of sizes. Chafing dishes and hotel pans are usually of standard sizes, so most of them will fit together properly. Occasionally for preparing foods but more often to hold cooked foods in steam tables, hot boxes, or electric or gas steamers. Frequently used to hold meats being marinated and for refrigerated food storage.

Plate mold. Deep rectangular metal mold, usually has hinged sides to facilitate removal of the plate. Special shapes may be available. Cooking plate en croute. Terrine mold. May be rectangular or oval, with a lid. Traditionally earthenware, may also be enameled cast iron. Cooking or molding terrines. Gratin dish. Shallow oval baking dish; ceramic, enameled cast iron, or enameled steel. Baking gratins. Ramekin. Round, straight-sided ceramic dish; comes in various sizes. Baking souffles; sometimes for molding frozen souffles; sauce cups; baked custard; baked or chilled puddings; gratins and a variety of other uses. Timbale mold. Small metal or ceramic mold. Molding individual portions of foods. Flexible silicone mold. Available in different sizes and shapes. Forming foods into a variety of shapes; can be used at high temperatures and for freezing.

Cake pan. Straight sided; available in various sizes and shapes. Can be used in a water bath. Baking cakes, cheesecakes, and some rolls. Springform pan. Similar to cake pan, but with separate bottom. Sides have springs to release for easy removal. Baking cakes.

Loose-bottomed tart pan. Shallow pan with removable bottom. Sides may be fluted or straight, and are generally shorter than those of pie pans. May be round, rectangular, or square. Baking tarts. Pie pan. Round pan with flared sides; deeper than tart pan; available in a variety of sizes. Baking pies and quiches. Loaf pan. Deep pan, usually rectangular. Sides may be straight or slightly flared. Baking breads and meatloaves. Pullman loaf pan. Rectangular pan with lid; produces flat-topped loaves. Baking specialty bread. Muffin tin. Pan with small, round depressions, which come in different sizes. Baking muffins and cupcakes. Bundt pan. Deep, round pan with tube in the center. May have ornate shapes. Creating a specific shape of cake, including chiffon and pound cakes. Tube pan. Deep, round pan with straight sides and tube in the center. Some are similar to springforms pans, with removable sides. Baking angel food cake, pound cake, or chiffon cakes.

Now let's discuss grinding, slicing, mixing and pureeing equipment. Grinders, slicers, and pureeing equipment all have the potential to be extremely dangerous. As these tools are essential for a number of operations, all chefs should be able to use them with confidence.

Most common tools for grinding, slicing, mixing, and pureeing. Blender: Consists of a base that houses the motor and a removable lidded jar with a propeller-like blade in its bottom. Speed settings for motor are in base. Jars made of stainless steel, plastic, or glass; available in several capacities. Excellent for pureeing, liquifying, and emulsifying foods. Food processor: Motor housed in base, separately from removable bowl, blade, and lid. May have extra disks for specialized cutting. Grinding, pureeing, blending, emulsifying, crushing, and kneading. With special disks: slicing, julienning, and shredding. Immersion blender/hand blender/stick blender/ burr mixer: Long, slender one-piece machine; like an inverted blender. Top houses motor, which generally runs at only one speed. Plastic handle with on/off switch extends from top of housing. Stainless steel driveshaft extends from motor and ends with blade, which is immersed in the food. Pureeing, liquifying, and emulsifying large batches of food directly in the cooking vessel.

Vertical chopping machine (VCM): Motor in base is permanently attached to bowl with integral blades. As a safety precaution, hinged lid must be locked in place before unit will operate. Grinding, whipping, emulsifying, blending, crushing large quantities of food. Food chopper/buffalo chopper: Food is placed in a rotating bowl that passes under a hood, where blades chop the food. Some have hoppers or feed tubes and interchangeable disks. Available in floor and tabletop models. Chopping large quantities of food; with special disks: slicing or grating. Food slicer/meat slicer: Carrier moves food back and forth against circular blade, generally made of carbon steel. Guard provides safety. Slicing foods in even thicknesses. Mandoline: Blades of high carbon steel. Levers adjust blades to achieve cut and thickness desired. Guard provides safety. Slicing, julienning, cutting gaufrettes and batonnets. Stand mixer: Electric machine has large detachable bowl of varying capacities (5-quart, 10-quart, 20-quart, 40-quart, etc.) Attachments: whip, paddle, dough hook. Bowl is locked in place and attachment rotates through batter or dough. Mixing, beating, whipping, kneading. Meat grinder: May be freestanding machine or attachment for a standing mixer. Should have disks of varying sizes, in general will have a feed tray and a pusher. Grinding stuffing sausage casings with attachment.

Moving on to the right refrigerator, cooler, and freezer equipment. Also the importance of refrigeration maintenance. The key to well-running refrigeration units is maintenance. A top condenser refrigeration unit is best suited for use in a bakery. A bottom condenser refrigeration unit is best suited near a deep fryer in your ghost kitchen. A mini fridge is not a basic type of refrigeration unit for your ghost kitchen.

Split door models are better because they minimize letting hot air in. They make it easy to be organized. They are more expensive. Prep table is the best type of refrigeration unit suited for the job, if you want to make a pizza. Always remember the more you have your refrigeration unit doors open, the more heat you let in and cold air out. So therefore it works twice as hard. This is while you have to keep it maintained or you could be paying $3K on a new refrigeration unit. And the best recoil.

Refrigeration maintenance guidelines: Regular cleaning and maintenance ensures that your refrigeration unit is staying energy efficient and keeping product cool. Whichever type of commercial refrigerator you choose, make sure to do the following tasks for best operation:

Wipe down the interior. Always wipe down the interior shelves and walls each week with a soft cloth, warm water, and manufacturer-approved cleaner. Remember to remove all products and place them in a cooler or another refrigeration unit. Wipe down the exterior each week, use a soft cloth, warm water, and manufacturer-approved cleaner to wipe down the exterior. Do not use abrasive or chlorine-based cleaners on stainless steel surfaces.

Clean the condenser coil. The condenser coil can accumulate lots of dust or grease in a commercial kitchen. At least once every three months, you should vacuum and clean the condenser coil. Check the gaskets. Check the door gaskets at least once a month. Wipe them down with a damp cloth to keep them clean. If you see any wear, splits, or cracks, have them replaced.

Finally, let's go back over the basics of refrigeration. Refrigerators are important units in a kitchen to safely store prepared foods and deliveries made by food service operations. Some basic guidelines about refrigerators are as follows: Refrigeration and freezing units should be regularly maintained and cleaned. These units should be equipped with thermometers to make sure that the temperature remains within a safe range. In general, refrigerators should be kept between 36° and 40°F. For refrigerating specific foods, use the following information for optimal storage: Meat and poultry 32° to 36°F, Fish and shellfish 30° to 34°F, Eggs 38° to 40°F, Dairy products 36° to 40°F, Produce 40° to 45°F.

Keep each category of food in separate refrigerators when possible. If storing multiple food categories in a single unit, divide the refrigerator into sections and store them separately in each section. The front of the refrigerator unit will be the warmest and the back the coldest.

Now you should be fully aware of how to start a ghost kitchen of what it really takes and behind the scene of the ghost kitchen reality. Before we finally end this chapter, I want to leave you with a few more opening start-up bonus tips. Also a checklist.

Some things to consider as an overview: Food cost. Menu developing. Timing for plate, take out, delivery. Cost of ingredients. Being on your feet, standing in one place periods of time. Confined in small places. Disaster areas of kitchen, cutting something wrong, overcooking, burning, undercook, hazardous, etc.

Sacrifices you have to make: home life and personal life. Prepare to work 14-hour days. A lot of people do it for the money. Don't simply get into it for just the money. Learn the craft. It is a lot of hard work and repetition. Long hours in the kitchen.

Every ghost kitchen budgets differently. If you're a personal chef, catering food company, food truck, restaurant, try a ghost kitchen.

Furthermore, conduct work with all kitchen stations. When tickets come in, you got to be ready. A good cook, a good leader. Learn timing in different stations. Expedite timing your hot line, cold stations. Cost of ingredients, how much items cost per portion and breaking down for menu. Buying food/purchasing and cooking it.

If it works, built on it, mix a little creative and fun. Managing staff, scheduling prep time, cleaning, ordering food. Make sure you know who your customers are, what they want and aware of your brand.

However, that means the pressure is on to run the kitchen as smoothly as possible. This starts with staffing the right employees and training them to strictly adhere to your operating model. As the restaurant staffing crisis persists, ghost kitchens need to take proactive measures to appeal to job-seeking cooks and gig workers.

Such steps include: Offering competitive pay and benefits. Being transparent about advancement opportunities. Fostering a healthy and supportive working environment. If these kitchens will have tremendous difficulty hiring reliable talent. Plus, great hires bring value due to easier training and a better chance of employee retention.

Finally, open your virtual doors. Mission accomplished! Once the previous actions in this how to start a ghost kitchen chapter have been completed, your ghost kitchen will be fully stocked, staffed, and prepared to serve hungry customers. And with ghost kitchens set to be a $1 trillion industry by 2030, there's no better time to build a foundation for this emerging restaurant trend.

Always remember your focus and power points. Financing. Doing budgeting and projections. Brand strategy. Logo. Business planning. Business model/mission statement. Research. Account planning. Focus group. Creative test. Advertisement. Insurance, if someone gets sick or employees. Sanitation, dry storage, frozen, refrigeration. Overhead. Renting your ghost kitchen space while your regular kitchen hours are closed down and offline. Signing an NDA (non-disclosure agreement). Year leasing vs. month-to-month or six month renting your ghost kitchen space.

In these following chapters to come I will assist to guide you on how to hone your ghost kitchen craft, not only to just help you learn the skilled craft to catch on. I will further help you with the following: location, menu developing, niche items/columns, delivery services, overhead, outsourcing, marketing, and finally franchising.

First I want to leave you with the details of my arrangement prior with a ghost kitchen so you can get a vivid realistic start-up figure. It is different virtual kitchens, cloud kitchens, ghost kitchens, or dark kitchens with various rates that run differently, so you must really do your thorough research. Do not be afraid to ask for a tour and guide with the very ghost kitchen location you are actually interested in or thinking about to consider your start-up point.

Most have you sign an NDA. The ghost kitchen I partner with was next to the university college within 10 minutes driving radius, which has to be for proper food delivery purposes some 10 miles. I put down a $5K deposit that was prorated for 60 days. I signed a 12-month lease and contract. After the 60 days my rent was approximately $3,700 per month.

They provided the kitchen equipment for my menu fryers, griddles, stovetops. They provided dry storage, coolers for my onions and potatoes, etc., dry storage, freezer space, and sanitation nightly.

They provided the POS (payment operation system) Otter and all the software with the delivery apps to the people ordering online directly to the notifications to the cooks of their selective order placements.

It was a kitchen for capacity of 4 chefs or cooks; however, in actuality for that small ghost kitchen space 2 cooks can really do it for the most part, and that saved me labor cost, time and money. The cooks were all paid $20 per hour. I had to start off with my kitchen management and food handler's permit before I got the cooks into the swing of things and basic training my own staff. Ghost kitchens most just provide the location, space, equipment and kitchen set-up. You have to find/hire your own cooks. Be wary of hiring friends and family because most of them do not think they can get fired or that they have to actually work-work.

The last thing is they provided me with the option to buy wholesale foods in bulk at their actual supplier. Or you can actually outsource from other food vendors of your choice and liking. The company also gave me an option to franchise with another one of their various locations nationwide. They provide data on your virtual dishes to help you further assist your menu development for the best success and profitable.

- Chapter 3 -

"Location"

Location: a place or position. Choose a location for your ghost kitchen. Selecting a location for a ghost kitchen harkens back to its concept. If the operation is simply a brand extension, it's completely acceptable to run the restaurant in an existing restaurant's kitchen, similar to what Chuck E. Cheese does with its ghost kitchen concept, Pasqua concept, Pasqually's Pizza & Wings.

This option makes the hunt for space, staff, and equipment much simpler. However, it runs the risk of overwhelming back-of-house staff and misleading customers when offering the same food from a different brand name. Selecting a unique location is the only option for new restaurateurs, and the choice on where to operate should be based on the availability of kitchen space, alongside a feasibility study to see if the concept would succeed in its proposed location.

When stuck on this step, here are some restaurant-finding tips to help get funds faster. A stone's throw from Koreatown and downtown and easily accessible from the 10 and 101 freeways, the unmarked warehouse proved to be an ideal location for a commissary, allowing drivers to quickly park and pick up delivery orders before shuttling them off to customers. Also college surrounding areas and freeway, and loop access busy areas, too. Highly populated areas.

When dealing with picking a unique location, make sure to do your homework and that it is beneficial, not just merely a cool concept or hot area. Some people choose locations based off their hearts. It could be from cultural backgrounds, trends, influences, and availability too. The key is to play it smart, do your due diligence on researching geographical locations and demographics. You can simply create a Google Analytics account online to gather the current data you need to assist you and an actualization of your reflection of location selection.

You also want to make sure that whatever ghost kitchen location you choose from shows you their current and past numbers before you sign any lease agreement and contracts. You also can be your own judge of locations, too.

Is it in a busy area, safety, median or high-income areas, and availability. Can all the delivery service apps get in-and-out to that specific ghost kitchen location accordingly without problems, long wait periods, and congestion parking? Then you want to check the availability of all the delivery services: DoorDash, GrubHub, Postmates, and UberEats. Sometimes certain apps don't have drivers availability 24/7 for certain locations. Especially if your location is remote like close to the mountains, high desert, or by a far military base.

Therefore, to your head and heart you may feel like, by your kitchen being remote location it's actually niche. However, please reconsider all the other prime factors involved. You are limited to an actual remote area to cater orders to because of the certain delivery guidelines, and regulation on a food's safe consumption time. You can only deliver so far and cannot go out of those restricted areas.

Next, your location accessibility is everything, first and foremost. Even if you are attempting to get funded and bring in investors on your location. Your business plan has to have and show accessibility. Parking lots and parking spots. Is it accessible? Is it a one-way street or dead end? Is the location on an industrial space that has a bad road or under heavy construction like in New York City? Can you double park? The traffic volume, obviously it will be higher volume traffic if your ghost kitchen does take-out and delivery, versus just delivery only for drivers. Some ghost kitchen locations like the one I was a part of, has all three options, from take-out, delivery, and dining-in. Some have an inside dining and outside patio to order and sit down and eat. I have seen drivers actually order in, sit down and eat, then pick up an order to deliver. Therefore, you have to go sightseeing, making sure you can see the location accessibility and the flow of its traffic. Look to see at its busy hours from breakfast, lunch, and dinner that it functions accordingly without too much blockage. Especially during rush hours and commute clogging. This is why some freeway close locations do swell, while others fail at certain times of the day, certain seasons like the holidays, or certain occasions like parades or marathons. It could be shut down often from construction, filming, homeless sweeps, weather conditions like snow, floods, and icy rain spots. These are all just some of the many things to take into consideration of location when dealing with accessibility overall. Again, most people just pick an ideal location without too much cognitive diligence and research of history and comps.

Higher median income accessibility vs. higher population accessibility. Basically the more money-earning areas vs. the heavily populated areas. Which one do you really want your ghost kitchen location to be accessible to? And again, there is also remote locations but that does limit you to a smaller food community. Accessible/accessibility means to be capable of being reached, or easy to communicate with and deal with.

My son Pierre works as a gig worker for UberEats as a side hustle. His delivery tips are way more in a few hours in Scottsdale, AZ, versus when he works the Phoenix metropolitan area. It takes him twice as longer to make the same amount. It's over 3 million citizens in Phoenix and 6 million total in the surrounding subdivisions. So you have a heavily populated busy area vs. Scottsdale, an elite, more higher median income.

My choice by experience I chose to start out my ghost kitchen partnership in Tempe, AZ, location next to ASU, which was a higher median income by $10K more than the Melrose Phoenix District location. The Melrose District location was more accessible to the main street for delivery drivers to swing thru and pick up orders. Whereas, the Tempe, AZ, ghost kitchen location was more in an industrial area access road, which made it a little bit more difficult to find for a first-time delivery driver, even with GPS.

Some locations are either off the grid or glitch on GPS, Google Maps, iOS, or Android devices and give delivery drivers wrong directions, spin them in a loop, or simply don't show for new drivers on their mobile device at certain locations. So you must also take this too into consideration with accessibility and location selections. Research is key and a mandatory practical principle in location assessment.

Now, I want to elaborate further on college surrounding areas for ghost kitchen location. The reason why a lot of the first father O.G. kitchens started opening up more commissary kitchens close to college campuses, was more college students ate out and ordered more food from delivery places before all the main popular apps you see streaming nowadays.

Therefore, if the college students ordered more food, that meant the delivery drivers and ghost kitchens made more money. This is why that demographic is more lucrative, and a hotbed for ghost kitchen locations.

You also need to look at the data and use it. Weigh in the factor that college students, bachelors, etc., all have themselves to provide for, vs. a 3-5 average family home that cooks whole meals on the regular. Family households may order delivery once or twice per week if they don't feel like cooking, did not have time or a special occasion, vs. a college student with roommates that may all order from your ghost kitchen location closest to their campus and surrounding areas.

The reason why downtown locations are popular, too, is from all the events, guests, hotels, office and bank executives, lawyers, judges, students, etc., all order from delivery apps, and if your ghost kitchen location is accessible to the downtown surrounding area, especially in a bigger city, it's definitely a plus for your location choice of selection.

Now, let's look forward at socio-cultural factors that regulate food. Biggest reason for people to eat. We eat for different occasions, like holidays or events. We eat on time, like breakfast, lunch, and dinner. Desire to eat comfortable, spicy, Mexican food, sweet foods, Italian food, etc. Appeal, depends on if it looks appetizing or not. Availability, certain time, economical, people may not have access. Cultural backgrounds. Food influences, experiences and curiosity of new food. Excitement phase. Geographical, certain regions.

Biological. The brain signals to the stomach when hungry. When full, leptin hormone, appetite-suppressing hormone.

Insulin, detects fat stored and sugar in our blood. Then you have metabolism, and genetic predisposition.

- Chapter 4 -

"Menu"

Eating is essential. As people we all must eat to live, survive, and have daily energy and calories. Which is why people are constantly on the prowl looking for food and new taste experience or to satisfy their cravings and hunger pains. Which is also why I want to reflect on the importance of your virtual menu featured for your ghost kitchen to the public. Presentation is everything and this is why menu development is your next step. In order to know what type of equipment to stock your ghost kitchen with, you must first design your menu and know what type of food you will need to cook for that commissary kitchen.

Menu is a list of foods that may be ordered at a restaurant, or a list of dishes that may be ordered.

How to open a ghost kitchen pivotal step is the menu and menu developing. Choose a concept and develop a menu first and foremost. A ghost kitchen concept needs to be unique, and appealing to off-premises diners. Successful ghost kitchens prioritize foods that are high-selling and feasible options for delivery and take-out. Popular delivery options include: Fried chicken dinners and sandwiches. Comfort food like mac 'n' cheese. Mexican cuisine like tacos, burritos, and chips and guacamole. Breakfast sandwiches.

On the other hand, some food options aren't suitable for delivery due to diner preference and their inability to travel well in to-go packing. These less-than-favorable delivery items include fried foods, eggs, and fine-dining entrees like steak. With these restrictions in mind, ghost kitchens should create a menu of options that are intended for consumption up to an hour after being prepared and will fare well with local tastes.

Your initial menu can also be limited in order to see what resonates with diners and optimize inventory management and kitchen operations. Having direct communication with audience and food community in real time.

Curate your own menu, theme, agenda, mixing creativity, design, entrepreneurship for a one-of-a-kind first-taste experience of first-time orders from your ghost kitchen menu service anyone is willing to taste test for experiment. However, the key is can you give them a great taste experience? Will they actually crave for or be a repeated customer order? People and foodies always looking for food and places they have not eaten at yet to tell their foodie community, which is a great and excellent word-of-mouth marketing tool for your ghost kitchen start-up and to be having trendy or popular menu dishes. Therefore, testing a new menu dish or adding a feature item to your existing menu that is well worth testing, because of the value you add to your menu board and ghost kitchen. The feedback and customer experience is priceless, because it's just like you collecting free data and marketing 101. One person tells another person or shares their new food taste and experience, and it spreads like wildfire. Especially throughout foodie community and local community, too. Essentially a good virtual menu is to serve hungry and hangry people to satisfy their craving taste or hunger pain.

Having a good professional photographer and graphic designer is important for your virtual menu board display for all the menu items listed to be high-resolution photos. So take into consideration, when you finally do create a menu item or dish, to invest in a professional to add value to your virtual menu. Remember presentation is everything, and first impression is always a lasting impression. The food industry is waking up to seeing they can eat from home and have a better kitchen and bathroom than restaurant.

Beyond meats fast food distribution. Impossible foods, or plant-based can be a better alternative choice but cost more expense. Therefore, make sure profit margins match cost. Doing a vegan menu is highly possible. You just need to know outsourcing can be expensive, and usually plant-based or alternative meats and foods usually have 5-8% mark-up. Whereas some imports 8-15% mark-up wholesale and distribution value. Again, remember to evaluate your cost per plant-based or imported vegan item to buy, labor help to cook, and retail price for your virtual menu. All your total cost, gross, net, and bottom-line profits, after overhead, employees, etc., should be exhausted in your business plan.

Now, let's get to the right-brain creative side. Creative dishes to create your first virtual menu concept to complete a whole menu for all the major delivery apps for the public communities to place orders and become regular clientele.

Let's be very creative, weigh our options, and create a think tank to get your mind going, and right brain stimulated to spark peak creativity positive brain flow. First step is time management. You have to make time out your daily schedule to set aside to begin to think aloud, or write down what you brainstorm. Especially when integrating foods or foodies' cultural backgrounds, brands, and traditional trends. Next step is to prioritize what type of dishes you want to make, the cost, cook time, and travel easy time of the dish for delivery. You do not have to be a creative genius to innovate your menu, just able to clear the clutter out your mind to be precise, very clear of knowing what you want to create, what you like, flavor, and what you love from your heart that you won't get tired of cooking, serving, smelling or tasting. The final step is to execute. All the ideas you think of that you write down, now it's time to act on them. Test them see what works and don't work. Do a mock menu template or PDF file menu template you can use to see how your menu options, prices, and sides look. Then always get a second set of eyes to see what they think and their first impression. Accept constructive criticism as a reality check, and positive feedback, that gives you hindsight and better overall perspective. You will always have critics, spectators, and naysayers in anything you do in life, especially new ventures. So stay focused on execution of your creative process. Do not overload your menu with cooking multiple dishes. You don't need to pump out 8 different main dishes to be successful like Burger King. Nothing too complex for yourself, kitchen staff, or delivery gig workers. Simplify, the less the cooking and less wholesale unit cost which makes a better profit margin versus overload on inventory, which makes it more to cook and prepare, and more time and cost-effective.

However, you can create as many virtual menus for your ghost kitchen if you can keep up with the demand you create and your cooks can keep up with all the orders putting them out timely. Menu multitasking can be effective or ineffective and disastrous. You can use them same side dishes like salad, fries, coleslaw, mashed potatoes, cookies, mac 'n' cheese, and soft drinks for menu multitasking. For example, at my ghost kitchen one of my virtual menus is called "Fish Stop" with multiple-flavored fried or glazed baked fish. The same concept of Wing Stop, except with fish. I offered a more healthier tilapia fish than the same ol' Alaskan cod and butter crisp plain fish batter. Then I have the "Chicken-N-Waffle Errthang" brand on my menu, where we offer chicken-n-waffle cupcakes, pizza, wraps, sandwiches, shake, and different types of chicken from jerk chicken, orange chicken, sesame chicken-n-waffle everything. Then we integrate most of our sides and drinks. So it's the same fries, mac 'n' cheese, coleslaw, etc. On Fish Stop virtual menu we have a jerk fish option and on Chicken-N-Waffle Errthang we offer a Jamaican-style jerk chicken-n-waffle menu option. Also list the chicken-n-waffle sweet cupcake on the Fish Stop virtual menu as a snack advertiser. So it's totally up to you and what works for you best menu multitasking. However, I wouldn't recommend it for first-timers without no prior ghost kitchen experience or kitchen management skills. Start slow and one at a time first, never bite off more than you can chew. Start slow and grow, success comes in steps. So again learn the craft and enjoy the process of endurance and dedication to balance your first ghost kitchen space. A lot of people have made grave mistake taking off running head-first into a brick wall, crashing their ghost kitchen with a Humpty Dumpty fall. I seen people shut down their ghost kitchen and still have to pay their leasing space rent. So you don't want to lose revenue or investments before you really get your feet wet over a faulty menu creative concept. Bad menu concepts equal bad results.

All menus must be clear, readable, not words too small or cluttered together. And a listed small definition of what's inside/included in that particular dish item of your virtual menu. For example, Jamaica-N-Waffles. Then listed underneath in a smaller font in quotes or unquotes would read: Jamaican-style jerk chicken-n-waffle maple syrup Belgium wrap.

Next, make sure the prices are set directly to the far right side from the listed item directly opposite on the far left side of the menu board. Make sure your price numbers are in a boldface font and a nice size so there is no confusion or misleading potential foodies or new consumers browsing in on your new virtual menu items and brand.

Decorate your menu. Create a nice logo for your new virtual kitchen brand. Playing with the template menu graphics or using Adobe Illustrated, Canvas, or Taylor brand is all fun to diy (do it yourself) to get first-draft ideas and looks before you pay a professional. And you do this final step after you already created your virtual menu items and listed prices. It's a fun collective effort afterwards and it feels like you awarding yourself as a victory lap in accomplishing the next huge step for your ghost kitchen. You have to know what you are cooking in your ghost kitchen and what your virtual menu features. An appealing menu such as an appreciation for niche and artisanal virtual menus in a trendy setting.

Make sure your virtual menu is appealing for all the scrolling eyes once you have complete your full menu concept and used the data analytics of the popular dishes on demand and the easier dishes to make that's also less time-consuming, or you can run out of the specialized cooking products. Keep these tips and factor into the equation of a nice menu layout.

Finally, after you took the proper steps to prevent poor performances, you can have a virtual menu ready to upload to whatever software and POS the ghost kitchen you choose to partner up with have. Menu development should be a fun task to complete your start-up ghost kitchen.

- Chapter 5 -

"Niche"

Niche: a specialized market; the ecological of an organism in a community especially in regard to food consumption. Also the situation in which a business's product or services can succeed by being sold to a particular kind or group of people.

Niches are very pivotal if you can find one or create one. If you can find something that has a special interest of demand, or if you can create something that hasn't been done successfully before, or even add/introduce a new feature to an already existing product that's niche. Your virtual menu can be niche or feature a niche dish or an actual niche side dish. The key is formulating to create or find a specific niche. You do not have to have the eye of the tiger necessarily. You do have to be very keen in particular with your niche column.

Like with your research and findings, along with again testing all your niche theories, concoction, and food integrations.

In the ghost kitchen industry or marketplace, we call a niche dish or niche menu outlier or outliers. An outlier is a statistical observation that is markedly different in value from the others of the sample. Or something as a geological feature that is situated away from or classed differently from a main or related body.

However, just because your ghost kitchen product placement is an outlier with niche items and ingredients does not mean instant success or exposure. A lot of people just starting in the ghost kitchen already have a great-grandma's recipe to integrate with a certain cultural background food tradition. Then build their menu and ghost kitchen foundation around that. Here are the hard facts. Popular items, dishes, and known brands sell and get selected to order more on the delivery apps than the outliers. Maybe you are an outlier who has a niche mac 'n' cheese popcorn chicken bowl. How does the public and the foodie community know your product exists or how it tastes? Versus them satisfying a craving they had before. Most people go with what they are familiar with, not unfamiliar with. People don't like to gamble their monies on new products they have not indulged in or consumed before. Some people, on the other hand, do and are willing to take a chance on your new niche product to the market if it looks appealing. It also takes a lot of marketing and brand integration to get people to try something new out their norm. The ghost kitchen I was a part of, the outlier made on average $30K per month minimum. Whereas, the popular food chains and brand-name piggyback kitchens made on average $60K per month minimum. So there is a huge difference, but this is not meant to discourage you. The world of foods is meant to differ in variety. So the discovery of niche product foods and dishes is very needed. It's your job to put it in demand heavy rotation, and have people craving and talking about it, just like the Popeyes niche chicken sandwich craze in 2019 that had the U.S. in a frenzy.

Go create a concept that nobody else has and run with it. Have a culture of food innovation. How to motivate people to execute, reconcept things/experiences. Use research, data to innovate, too. Innovation and ideation is an opportunity. Be tenacious and consistent. Help to engage people and get them to be more involved in making a difference in the food industry niche revolution. The world is about to change!

Think about something new. Your solutions, strategies have to change.

If you self-identify as a "foodie," then you know how important it is to find the best restaurants, food trucks, and delivery services to satisfy every craving, especially variety of outliers/niche. Imported or exotic taste, expensive taste. Then you have the sea of sameness, the same ol' thing .The sea of kitchens, food trucks, restaurants, etc., be uniquely different.

Psychologically effect, the cognitive effect food, the sensory area of the brain, which trigger cues like visual to response and signal the gut to growl, crave, and roar. Food icons, cravings, food obsession, food addiction, healthier food culture/choices. Attracting customer attention to be profitable.

Concoction dishes, recipes, mixing and matching. Now, I will give you some bonus tips on the niche rules of engagement and how to finesse a special niche, and curate the market. Innovate with reality.

For example, let's use my two food menu concepts. Even though I was renting one ghost kitchen space, I was still cooking for two different virtual menu brands for people to order from their apps. Basically two different food concepts.

So with one I was able to do as a concoction, or you can think of it as a hybrid, because I integrated a popular food concept with an outlier concept, too. To further elaborate I mixed a mainstream popular dish with a new niche twist. Then curated my market in an already existing mainstream market for the popular demand item. Introducing a main dish with new entrees or new taste and styles of ingredients, too. Converting cold traffic by enticing them with new delights to be open to click your order now, shopping food cart.

Therefore, with my Chicken-N-Waffle Errthang brand, the mainstream food concept is chicken-n-waffles, which therefore is not classified as an outlier technically. However, the niche part is where I actually integrated "Errthang" (Everything). So basically introducing a new niche chicken-n-waffle maple syrup pizza, jerk chicken-n-waffles, orange chicken-n-waffles, chicken-n-waffle wraps, chicken-n-waffle cupcake, and chicken-n-waffle shake or soda for drink, which isn't just genius niche, it caters to the chicken-n-waffle lovers, foodies, audience, and communities on and offline. This is how you emerge or integrate a niche/outlier food concept with a popular or trendy one. And to curate a new market for a new taste. Again, you want to get your unique concept in demand or heavy rotation.

Now, on the other hand, was my second virtual menu and food brand named Fish Stop. The Fish Stop is a fish and chips brand. However, it's not the tradition fish and chips brand. We offered multiple kinds and style of fish, and niche in multiple flavors of fish, and flavored French fries, too. Again, basically the Wing Stop of fish. Therefore, technically that classified as an outlier food concept and virtual menu, because everything was a curated niche concept, which meant you had to convert and stop cold traffic online, offline, and introduce them to your new food brand, and market a new food brand. Like, Fish Stop has a dry flavored fish or a wet flavored fish, and mango habanero hot flavored fries, but how does the market or world of foodies and restaurateurs know it exists? As an outlier the 80/20 rule exists. Meaning 80% of your niche market is looking for your specialized food menu item. And the other 20% don't have no idea your niche exists. Which may be willing to try your new niche dish. Or you can convert them just by raising brand awareness, which we will get into the dynamics of brand awareness and building in the upcoming chapters, too.

Do not be afraid to spark your niche dream dish or taste you always wanted to bring to the world to tastes. Outliers food existence is admirable.

- Chapter 6 -

"Delivery Service"

Delivery: the act of taking something to a person or place: something that is delivered. A person who delivers goods to customers from a store, restaurant, or ghost kitchen.

For delivery service options, first develop a distribution strategy. Ghost kitchens need an ironed-out plan for how food will get to customers. The first decision is whether to offer direct customer pick-up. Most ghost kitchens forgo this option to streamline the process for drivers and spend less time and money perfecting restaurant's façade.

However, there are financial benefits to offering pick-up or drive-thru options. For example, if a third-party delivery app charges a 30% commission for delivery, offering a 10-15% discount for pick-up ordered directly from the business can save the restaurant and the guest money. The other decision is which delivery methods to utilize.

Using one or more delivery partners like UberEats, GrubHub, or DoorDash means order volume will almost certainly be higher than if they were not used. However, not every delivery app is right for every ghost kitchen, so third-party options should be evaluated for their merits and drawbacks before signing up.

It's important to factor commission costs into menu prices when partnering with these services. As an alternative, ghost kitchen business can use in-house delivery solutions that eliminate third-party commission fees.

The drawback, however, is that restaurants sacrifice exposure and opportunity for new customer acquisition inside a third-party's marketplace. These first-party delivery solutions might also be hosted via a third-party delivery app, which further simplifies the back-end management of this software.

Regardless of how the food gets to customers, it's imperative that meals are sent out of the kitchen in take-out-friendly packaging and containers that preserve intended temperature and keep specific foods separated until they're ready to be consumed.

Now, equipped with rivers of data provided by app users, tech-based delivery companies can home in on the demand for specific cuisines within geographic areas, even going as far as approaching struggling food businesses with branded concepts that can be tacked onto their existing menu with minimal effort. Even IHOP has a ghost kitchen under a different brand, same food.

The only way you can have success is saying what's next. Delivery can be outsourced with private third-party delivery options, too. You cannot get into the ghost kitchen atmosphere without thinking about labor or distribution delivery services. Accountability, make sure you follow up to your commitments. When you don't, that allows failure.

First you must really decide between offering pick-up to customers vs. drive-thru options or doing delivery. Or possibly all 3 options which would mean more revenue and more traffic with packed parking spots. With direct customer pick-up and having a drive-thru option to your ghost kitchen, it will save you time and money as long as you can keep up with the demand. Which they both add value to your ghost kitchen, not just revenue, but for brand and customer experience, too.

Next, you must also take into the consideration of timeliness of all three distribution options of take-out, pick-up, and delivery. The turnover rate from the notification to the cook time of each food item ordered and the pick-up, drive-thru, delivery ETA, too. Getting food out on time for delivery drivers is everything because it can get kitchens bad reviews and delivery services platforms or third-party private vendor apps penalized for late service fees. Some even have marketing perks such as they guaranteed on-time delivery or you get your food order free of charge. GrubHub runs these types of specials but all of the delivery service apps have some type of promotion and special features from low rates to delivery incentives, because of all the new delivery service tech-base boom. Especially after the 2020 COVID-19 pandemic quarantine lockdown where citizens were confined to their homes with loss of many jobs and big entities forced to shut down and stay in home, too.

Also on getting orders out timely, it's about the specific ghost kitchen's location and accessibility of not having delivery drivers wait, get penalized, or congested parking/traffic. Again, a lot of these apps have time perks. So your delivery drivers sit and wait time shouldn't be long at all. If it's over 5 minutes that's considered too long. It should be ready all orders by the time the delivery driver pulls up to your ghost kitchen and checks in to pick up your order to deliver to the consumers. It typically should be a smooth transition of an in-and-out process. I will elaborate more of this from inside of a delivery driver's aspect, too.

Then you have your to-go packaging, seal stamps or sticker on food with your logo and trademark ghost kitchen name and design on it. Basically to ensure safe delivery and safety of the delivered goods, which shows the food package was not tampered with long as the stickers, staples, or tape and receipt is not altered, broken, or breached in any shape or fashion. Which again, all ensure quality of services for the consumer orders. You must design your logo and packaging. You can register them with your local Secretary of State or the USPTO (United States Patent & Trademark Office). With to-go packing remember less-than-favorable delivery items include fried foods, eggs, and fine-dining entrees like steak. They don't travel well and have food consumption life short time periods stipulated.

Now, I want to explain to you the delivery process for drivers and pick-up. Then describe to you the delivery driver's duties.

When a delivery comes in with UberEats, it tells the driver how long the overall delivery should take. How many miles you'll be driving, your expected pay, and the ghost kitchen or restaurant's name and exact location.

You have about 15 seconds after the notification as a delivery driver to accept or reject the delivery. After you accept it, you'll see the customer's name, what they ordered far as food items, drinks, and sides, and finally their contact information and the contact information for the restaurant.

There is also a button to press to let UberEats know that the food is not done when you arrived to the restaurant. As a delivery driver you can also change your mind after you accept the delivery if you decide you want to cancel. You can message or call the customer at any time.

When you get the food from a ghost kitchen, and you drop it off at the delivery destination for the customer, you have the option of taking a picture of the sealed food items in the bag, or just leaving a note, and leaving at the door. This is just to show for confirmation of delivery purposes, and so you're not stuck awaiting for people to get home or answer the door for 10 additional minutes pigeonholed from your other delivery orders timely.

You can also accept new deliveries when you're on the current delivery. Sometimes you will have to pick up orders from different ghost kitchens and restaurants or the same ghost kitchens and restaurants. However, I do want to warn you as a delivery driver, you can get penalized, also your account suspended temporarily from the major delivery service apps and platforms. For instance, I have seen a delivery driver at the ghost kitchen in Tempe, AZ, pick up two different orders, one for UberEats and the other GrubHub, multitasking. Now of course a delivery driver will make more money, tips, and perks this way, but when you cannot deliver to two places at the same time in opposite directions, one gets late notification and delivery time max. Therefore, you get penalized and account possibly suspended, so please keep all this into account.

Then you have delivery service perks, which many of the delivery service apps and third-party private vendors have included. Like UberEats once you become a diamond driver, you get perks such as: Discounted dental/vision. TurboTax self-employed discount. Free health savings account. 100% tuition coverage with ASU online. Priority support. 25% off car maintenance. Costco Gold Star membership. 25% fuel rewards.

It is also something called U cars for gig workers/delivery drivers rentals. It's like $375 per week usually for like a Prius rental for all delivery service workers. This is a perk because these rental cars are great on gas and some environment-friendly with alternate fuel such as electric and solar friendly.

Now, I will further describe the duties of a delivery driver, and explain the skills and education required to obtain a job as a delivery driver.

Duties, delivery drivers. Load and unload their orders. Follow all applicable traffic laws. Keep their cars/trucks and associated equipment clean and in good working order. Accept payments and tips for the service. Handle paperwork such as receipts or delivery confirmation notifications.

Necessary education or training. Delivery drivers and gig workers typically have to be 18 or 21 years of age to enter their occupations with a high school diploma or equivalent. They must have a driver's license from the state in which they work. They must undergo one month or less of on-the-job training.

Important qualities and skills. Customer service skills: When completing deliveries, drivers are often interacting with customers and should make a good impression to ensure repeat business. Hand-eye coordination: When driving, delivery drivers need to observe their surroundings while simultaneously operating a complex machine. Math skills: Because delivery drivers sometimes take payment, they must be able to count cash and make change quickly and accurately, especially with third-party delivery service vendors or private ones.

Patience: When driving through heavy traffic congestion, delivery drivers must remain calm and composed. Sales skills: Drivers are expected to convince and encourage customers to purchase new or different products from them. Especially for third-party delivery service drivers. Speaking ability: Drivers must comprehend English well enough to read road signs, prepare written reports, and communicate verbally with public officials and law enforcement officials. Visual ability: To have a driver's license, delivery drivers must be able to pass a state vision test.

Remember the delivery drivers represent the delivery service app/company and the ghost kitchen chain. More products means more money. Sell and deliver their products, provide friendly and attentive service to their customers they deliver to and engage with daily.

Lastly, because of the Russia and Ukraine war, it has been a domino effect, causing inflation globally. Because of the recession it's a spike/hike in prices, especially delivery service prices. Any time the gas prices inflate or increase, delivery services are sure to follow inevitably. As of today, June of 2022, from the inflation of the U.S. the delivery apps are up 3% surcharge fees. I must discuss this to make you aware of all the odds and ends of joining a ghost kitchen to give you a vivid perspective to look thru a wider business lens, to prepare you for start-up success, not failure. These spikes come and go, prices increase and decrease regularly. You need to make sure your ghost kitchen delivery service can sustain thru it all, because it's part of the economy business realm.

Delivery has become the new norm and delivery service platforms mainstream and a fortune. Circuit is a new popular third-party delivery service the ghost kitchen and home kitchens use.

- Chapter 7 -

"Overhead"

In this chapter we will discuss another important aspect that's overlooked start-up at a ghost kitchen, which is called overhead. The best way to put it is to expect the unexpected always. You cannot under-mind overhead in any business or business venture even if it's a virtual business. When I started up my own tattoo shop I assumed overhead, but it wasn't nowhere close to what I actually estimated. My original numbers were way off that I included in my business plan. I could not get a bank loan, so I had to lease a tattoo shop small space, just like the ghost kitchen. However, the ghost kitchen's overhead was twice the amount of the tattoo shop's overhead. This is why you must be aware of overhead going into the ghost kitchen industry. Especially when using a private commissary kitchen that third-party leases its spaces out to for cooking vendors, who outsource or link out to their own delivery services. These are not the typical traditional ghost kitchens or cloud kitchens, but they still exist and pump out orders hourly. Therefore, overhead for your kitchen business plan, allow 10 to 15%. And overhead for a more private mom-and-pop ghost kitchen space without the more exclusive up-to-date software and POS or Otter system, you should have it as 15-20% more for overhead. Without the big tech-based companies behind your ghost kitchen, the more you have to do organically working in the business, versus on the actual business. Which equals more overhead cost.

Let's review what overhead consists of. Overhead: cost for rent, heat, electricity, etc., that a business must pay and that are not related to what the business sells. Business expenses not chargeable to a particular part of the work or product.

Some examples of overhead that exist and can occur anytime in your ghost kitchen operation experience: Oven ranges, boilers, fryers can go out unexpectedly at any given time. Even if you followed all service and regular maintenance guidelines. Including any heavy equipment, too. Sometimes it can be a power surge and the temporary power outage can shock your heavy equipment and blow fuses, leaving your machinery down.

We had a power outage in the kitchen facility that caused our refrigerator to clunk out. The backup generator and facility emergency power sources were all backed up and running. Even the freezers were up and running, too. This caused a lot of overhead. Having to call a refrigerator emergency repair handyman service. The cost of replacing all the thawed food and inventory products, plus possibly having to replace the whole refrigeration unit as a whole if unrepairable. The labor cost for employees cleaning up, and the cost of loss daily or weekly income until the refrigeration unit or heavy machinery is fixed. From just this one example it can hinder your ghost kitchen start-up success and dampen your daily expected earnings with driven spiraling lost wages. Thus, overhead is expected.

Another prime example of unexpected overhead in a ghost kitchen facility is product shortage. Running out of goods. Especially if you have imported items or niche ingredients, too. One time it was a lettuce recall, so no lettuce was coming in. Next it was a bird flu and a cow disease where it all had to be thrown out immediately and inventory backlogged. It could be for CDC health reasons, crisis, or scares. If you have an ancient Chinese secret recipe where it imported from China only, and China goes on a quarantine or the U.S. prohibits

China imported/exported traded goods, you will again be stuck with overhead from taking your selected special niche items off your virtual menu. And, again, lost wages.

Therefore, you need to be extremely cautious with planning properly for overhead expenses. You should leave room not just in your business plan for overhead, but in capital or savings, such as emergency funds. If you are part of a ghost kitchen partnership and under an assigned leasing agreement, it's still subject to change. Let's say it's an environmental effect or cause, like the environment is getting hotter everywhere from global warming. The ghost kitchen warehouse facility bricks can heat up too, causing hotter inside working conditions and spoil foods too. Therefore, your overhead can increase with an extra $100-$200 in A/C accommodation bill from the facility. If the facility has to upgrade a system, integrate a special feature or water bill goes up, they will include it on taxing your rent kitchen space. So if you're paying $3,700 per month leasing, it could be a slight gap increase upwards towards $3,800 to $4,000 easily.

Now, speaking of water bills and water systems. We discussed in previous chapter about the importance of having potable water in your ghost kitchen facility to cook and cleanse with.

However, it is just as important when selecting your ghost kitchen location that you include water sources. Meaning where is the ghost kitchen's main water source coming from? Then check the liability. Is the renovated old facility having old pipes, plumbing issues, and fresh potable water supply pipes? There are a few ghost kitchens that run into water supplies, water treatment, and plumbing pipe issues. Especially in some of the many rural areas, but urban areas are not exempt, and can be problematic, too. This is all overhead that you cannot always necessarily avoid, but if you do your due diligence, you can cut that overhead price in half by preventing leasing in kitchen space with bad plumbing or bad water source history. Once you understand the actualization of the importance of overhead, you will tame enthusiasm that's going to make your ghost kitchen concept and business work. The proper preparation involving overhead is simply to have emergency funds available to back up any sudden kitchen crisis. And the strategy is to avoid any rundown ghost kitchen antics. Like if it's too rundown and more of a risk and liability than an actual business venture, you should most likely turn the other way and look elsewhere. Or you will be investing in your life savings or family monies into a huge overhead that you did not calculate. Just because you got into a ghost kitchen for a significantly lower rate to lease the space does not mean you won on overhead coast, too. Sometimes higher rent space means higher amenities and it's worth it. You definitely get what you pay for. Remember an underlying factor: just because it's a cheaper rent space for your ghost kitchen, does not guarantee it will not be a shitshow and you coughing up tons of overhead. Some overhead can literally get over your head where have to choose whether tapping into your personal checking or savings account, or option B—shutting your ghost kitchen operation doors down, and virtual menu officially offline and all the delivery service apps or third-party vendors. Overhead is considered a factor in any and all business.

- Chapter 8 -

"Outsourcing"

Outsourcing is yet another exclusive essential to a ghost kitchen existence. It can be very beneficial if used or even add value to your existing ghost kitchen, too.

Outsource: to send away (some of a company's work) to be done by people outside the company. Or to procure (as some goods or services needed by a business or organization) under contract with an outside supplier. Like you decided to outsource some back-office operations, but for the ghost kitchen you will outsource product, equipment, software, delivery services, and possibly employees. All can be outsourced strategically. Also outsourcing your prepackaging to-go orders and seals, napkins, cup lids, take-out friendly containers that's intended to keep temperatures.

Source suppliers. For restaurants that already have a trusted food supplier, it's simple to utilize that same supplier for a new ghost kitchen concept, if the supplier offers bulk discounts. It's even easier to gain a quick profit from the ghost kitchen, as lower food costs means higher margins for virtual menu items.

New restaurants, however, might struggle to find the same discounts. Which is why starting off with a limited-size menu is so important. Ordering a surplus of a few ingredients (rather than a smaller amount of multiple ingredients) streamlines kitchen operations and creates an opportunity for high-volume discount from suppliers.

Shopping around to find a supplier to outsource who offers the best value (i.e., quality for the price) gives ghost kitchens the financial breathing room they need when starting out. Look at what's the value you're going to add to your ghost kitchen. Figure out a way to scale. You can use farm-fresh food, and find low cost just like Whole Foods does with its fresh organic food concept. You can apply the same principles to a ghost kitchen concept if you can find the correct company/farm vendor to outsource your ghost kitchen with, too.

Outsource equipment. Get the right technology. Like all restaurants, ghost kitchens need a suite of tools and technology in order to run smoothly. Naturally this means POS software, as well as an integration system like ItsACheckMate or Otter to sync online ordering directly to the POS.

If orders are accepted directly from guests, online ordering software is a must, alongside a restaurant analytics platform to easily analyze sales and produce actionable insights to improve the business.

Finally, online loyalty programs can incentivize first-time diners into becoming repeat customers for a restaurant by rewarding take-out purchases with discounts or free items.

The key in outsourcing is if it can simplify the process or streamline the process in your food kitchen, from any and all processes in the ghost kitchen, not just food vendors, POS, software, and equipment. The most thing I see outsourced in a ghost kitchen is food source, especially the fresh produce. A lot of ghost kitchens have their own wholesale vendors for bulk that's cheaper than if you flat-out did your own outsourcing for starters. Look at it like this: a ghost kitchen facility gets a better wholesale deal price per unit or per pound of food products to cook, because they are the supply chain to the whole ghost kitchen facility. You may partner with a ghost kitchen that have 6 to a dozen other units in that same facility that they supply and offer their wholesale vendor and prices inexpensive. It's option and up to you if you so choose to outsource with your own private vendor or niche wholesale vendors. It just may be more cost-effective because you are not buying in super bulk like your ghost kitchen wholesale supply chain is doing by the volume. In order to achieve a wholesale deal of this magnitude, you have to buy in quantity. However, there are still many perks from outsourcing, with your current ghost kitchen partner chain or without them. For me personally, it was a cut-and-dry decision to make. I chose to utilize the ghost kitchen sources they had into play, from their food wholesaler distribution to their Otter software and POS, their virtual menu development, their delivery service platforms into place, and their analytics. It all helped for a smooth transition from start-up, until I got the swing of things, then I felt more comfortable of outsourcing new niche products, ingredients, and new menu developing. You can outsource new logos, packaging, marketing, rideshares, and private vendors and ghost kitchen consultants.

- Chapter 9 -

"Marketing"

Marketing: the act or process of selling or purchasing in a market; the process or technique of promoting, selling, and distributing a product or service; an aggregate of functions involved in moving goods from product to consumer.

Creating a marketing plan: A detailed marketing strategy should touch upon all of the ways a ghost kitchen will stand out in its market, acquire new customers, and retain existing ones. There is a sea of general restaurant marketing tips on the internet, but here are some marketing ideas specifically for ghost kitchens.

Create a restaurant website to boost SEO discoverability. Allow curious diners to learn more about the business and link to online ordering options. Build a social media presence and promote social accounts on order receipts. Food pics, discount codes, and menu specials are quick and easy fodder for filling up a social media feed.

Promote the restaurant on delivery apps by paying a premium to place higher than competitors on customer searches. Although financially unsustainable, it's a good practice for newly opened restaurants to build awareness and acquire new customers.

Fill out a marketing plan unique to the ghost kitchen staffing and training. The good news for ghost kitchens is they require less staff than their full-service counterparts do. With no need for servers, order-takers, or counter workers, employees can focus solely on cooking, packaging, and organizing orders for pick-up.

Introduce your brand, learn everything about market. You create a marketplace, you learn from the marketplace, then you try to pick out things that you can execute better than what's available. It's the same way Amazon and Netflix operate. But given organizational complexity that makes up the ghost kitchen economy, it's fair to wonder how much money trickles down to individual restaurant owners.

In marketing, what message are you sending? Food and food culture define you a bit more than it will appear at first.

Constructive failure: Great plans and marketing ideas that didn't work or make the cut, failed. Sometimes timing, if it wasn't ready for the market, the over and done pile.

Food culture: a connection with your public and foodies. Ads dictate what we eat and crave from the visual cues that plants into our subconscious, which signals the gut to the satisfactory craving. The same way like a highway sign tells you food ahead, stop at next exit in a few miles. You indirectly turn off the exit ramp to feed your visual cue and craving. It's lifestyles with certain cultures/heritages, concoctions of mixing food styles and culture to market with your brand.

Popeyes disrupted the marketplace cooking/adding a new spicy chicken sandwich on their menu. It was niche for Popeyes, which spiraled/buzzed into a viral and social media phenomenon. You can bring something new to the marketplace or introduce an innovation of foods to disrupt the market.

Awareness, presence of a new food chain to community. Interactive. Like using website, blogs, social, and mobile. Media. Planning, purchasing, and testing new media. Research. Account marketing planning, focus marketing group, and creative test. Advertisement. Product placement,

TV broadcast/podcast, social media paid ads, and print like flyers, buttons, signs, or digital billboards.

Tap into the foodie community and market smart. How you market your virtual menu and ghost kitchen delivery service is time management, organize, prioritize, and strategize. Do not put your money, time, or staff time doing marketing promo if it's not working. For example, you don't want to invest in a ton of flyers for your food kitchen, passing them out to the delivery service workers for deliveries, then once you go on break you see a ton of colorful food kitchen flyers wasted all over the parking lot spaces. Do not get the wrong idea. Flyers is guerrilla marketing 101 with ground and pounding, because you can pay people to pass out flyers in urban communities that have high populations from car windshields, to shopping malls/plaza, and apartment complexes. Even laundromats work with flyers. It's all brand awareness and building. One person tells a friend and so on to spread word of mouth. Then one turns into 10, 10 turns into 50, 50 turns into 100 people that's now aware of your virtual menu and ghost kitchen brand thru word-of-mouth marketing. It's just like the power of social media and your brand going viral organically with no paid ads, just the power of one person's testimonial post from their food experience with your new food chain to market. Then someone shares, retweets, or reposts it organic, and 10 more people turns into 100 people and so on until your brand buzzing in the food market community on all social platforms. And it all is highly possible with the right food products and menu, also the right marketing structure and plan into play.

You can become what I call a marketgineer (marketing-engineer). Just like Ye (Kanye West) does with his Yeezy's music, and merch lines, with other big brand name companies. Outsmart the food market. Be disruptive, niche, an outlier, cross-brands, etc. It is a such thing called being a food genius. Like Kanye West you can apply your marketgineer skills to appeal to your food brand market. Do not be afraid to think outside the box and spark right-brain creativity to market any food chain brand you formulate. Think outside the typical marketing norm, and all those marketing templates they have online. Because those are all someone else's power marketing points, or market strategies. The best ones are the ones you organically germinate yourself. I'm not saying come up with huge marketing ploy schemes at all. I am saying to relax, take your time to think properly, plan to dig deep within self to visualize your brand mantra, mission statement, awareness, and building naturally. It should come and flow naturally if this food product and brand is something that you are passionate about or love to truly do. If not and you're just in the ghost kitchen marketplace to follow the money train and trend, then it may be 10x higher harder to organically come up with peculiar marketing ploys and pitches. Whereas, you may have to hire somebody to market for you or pay a known marketing firm to do so. However, even paying big-name marketing companies or ads doesn't guarantee the instant turnaround result you demand, you may only get back 5 to 10% what you invest. They see, but don't order or click to your website and virtual menu. It's risk and reward.

Marketing is the activities that are involved in making people aware of a company's products, making sure that the products are available to be bought, etc.

Now, marketable is able to be sold; wanted by buyers or employers. A fit to be offered for sale in a market. Be careful with pick food or things that is not marketable. You also have marketable securities and marketable skill or marketable capitalization, too.

Marketable is really being aware and know the market value of a niche or product. For example, say you realize that the cultural fry bread heritage recipe you enjoyed making traditionally, were highly sought and marketable. So you began selling them online to the fry bread foodie community, trying to turn an innovation or food concoction into a marketable product, brand or franchise.

There is also a such thing as called market demand, where you're forced to market. Also shock value from demand by default or limited products. An example of this was like the rapper 2-Chainz, he said in one of his hip-hop lyrics, "When they going to make that Bentley truck!" which had the whole hip-hop industry going viral. So much buzz, Bentley actually heard the market demand. They listened to what the people wanted increased value pushing the market demand in scope. A few years later Bentley released an exclusive Bentley truck, supplying the demand. Now Bentley trucks are in the market rotation to stay. And created market value that has other foreign luxury handcrafted sport vehicles add their truck version to the market space to capitalize on the market damn truck craze.

You have to know the importance of not just watching or following the market, but listening to the marketplace, too. Engage with your audience, social media, and foodie communities thru their taste experience from your ghost kitchen food brand. Consumers always tell you what they want, love, like, or dislike. Engage, read the comments and all the reviews, including the bad ones to problem-solve and evolve. Market direct to your food consumer needs, save time and money.

- Chapter 10 -

"Franchising"

In the final chapter of this *How to Start a Ghost Kitchen Delivery Service*, we will end discussing most restaurateurs dreams of food brand franchising. Most foodies and business owners, not just as ghost kitchen owners, all have an ultimate goal to franchise their brand and business.

Let's finish this last chapter telling you what franchising is, the difference, and how to franchise. Franchising can take years and extremely difficult within the first 1 to 5 years. Franchising can be fun, but it can be complex with brand build, and brand evolving, with brand repetition. All the ups and downs or highs and lows of the food industry, and the economy like government shutdowns or inflations, wars, etc.; it all factors into the equation when attempting to franchise your food kitchen brands.

Franchise: the right to sell a company's goods or service in a particular area; also a business that is given such a right. Or to grant a franchise to. Now a franchiser is a person who grants the franchise. A franchisee is one who gets rights to sell company goods. And finally a franchisor is one who grants both.

Think of franchising like licensing to the public to use your products or company. For example, Pepsi is a franchise brand where other companies pay a license fee to use their brand and products.

Once your food brand becomes popularly known from your city, state, or nationally, and possible even globally, then you can franchise your food business to the public, companies, vendors, schools, etc., which is called or named a franchisee.

Any companies you see with a whole bunch of different food chains, stores, or business, from Subway, McDonald's, Wal-Mart to Nike, Polo, and Oakley; all are typically franchises, where they will grant a franchise/rights to sell the company's goods, service, or brand. The franchisor is the company to give out or allow the franchisee, remember.

Now, for you to acquire the public to see value in your ghost kitchen food brand, whether niche or not, it has to be working, and successful. Before they will be a family franchisee partner to sign a franchising license contract, they will need to see your annually, quarterly, and monthly gross net profit margins and actualize profit after loss wages, labor and food cost, etc.; that record/report for the last 5 years and all the company's past and existing data. Especially the menu analytics and repeat customers data.

Typically to buy into a restaurant or a food chain brand franchise, you would need a franchisee fee and minimum deposit which can be from $20,000 to $500,000, it just depends on the franchisor. Then they require for you to have a new location or an ideal location, they will come walk thru and inspect. They want to see if the location is a good, safe, and clean place to represent their franchisement. Remember it's their brand so they have a right to accept or reject you as a potential franchisee applicant. You will have to buy enough inventory of their brand, from their supply wholesale food chain, or private vendors. Then they want to make sure you have enough revenue to cover their franchise monthly fees, too. Sometimes if it's a restaurant you would have to use their typical layout floor plan style. Like Subway and McDonald's all have the same layout at most locations. With a ghost kitchen, of course it will be the same franchise virtual menu items with the ghost kitchen layout suited for what you cooking on your menu.

You can look at an actual ghost kitchen as a franchise, too, that franchises its commissary kitchen space to you under contract of the lease, using all their supplies, resources, software, delivery service apps, sanitation, freezer, dry storage, and equipment. Most ghost kitchen facilities are owned by the company, but 15 are franchised ghost kitchens, like Cloud Kitchens.

Therefore, you can look at franchising a few different ways. A special privilege granted to an individual or group; especially the right to be and exercise the powers of a corporation. Also the right or license granted to an individual or group to market a company's goods or services in a particular territory; also a business granted such a right or license. Franchising can also apply to sports. The right of membership in a professional sports league. A team and its operating organization having such membership. Music producer DJ Khaled is set to franchise 150 ghost kitchens globally, he said, to stay ahead of the wave and new trend.

How to start your own ghost kitchen franchise, you first need to have a ghost kitchen success. From vibrant menu success, timely orders getting cooked and delivered in timely fashion. Great reviews, great brand and virtual menu concept, and your numbers are up, and increasing with your profit turnover rate or better known as ROI (return on your investment). Any potential franchisee is going to want to see the ROI and all the numbers. Your food chain brand should have a well-known reputation for good quality food, service, and experience. It should be a welcoming friendly environment. Remember some people do it for the actual experience your food service provides, and food is family, culture, and a social medium, too. Then your virtual food menu have to be ringing, having some type of buzz in its space. Like great marketing to keep people talking, sharing, and wanting to experience your brand great taste or items all. Again, this does not happen overnight, but over a grace period. An example, it is a Phoenix small mom-and-pop chain called Lolo's Chicken-N-Waffles, which grew exponentially after the first 5 years. It franchises with 4 Phoenix locations, a Las Vegas, Omaha, and counting. So dreams do become a reality, I have witnessed it with my own eyes. Your ghost kitchen food brand does not have to go public with an IPO (Initial Public Offering) with an opening on Wall Street before you can franchise or be a franchisor.

The ghost kitchen team I was a part of, too, had options to franchise and to open up more locations. It was just the two Tempe and Phoenix locations. They had options from all thru the whole state of California, Texas, NYC, Atlanta, Colorado, Chicago, D.C., and Boston. Once they see all your analytics and success, they want to keep you going in the ghost kitchen business. In the state of Arizona marijuana is legal for recreational, so the ghost kitchen was waiting to get approved to also do the marijuana delivery service on the apps, too. Which is another turn of the heels, and a lucrative cash cow people are going into a frenzy to tap in. Once you build a good partnering relationship with your ghost kitchen owner/management team, they will give you first usage rights when they integrate a new innovation or add on to the kitchen chains.

You're officially educated and ready to get started on your ghost kitchen success. I hope you enjoyed me taking the time out to sit down and manually handwrite this how-to book from my ghost kitchen experience to save you time, money, and from making big first-timer or rookie mistakes or bad reviews. I wanted to take you thru a commissary kitchen and explain how it all works A-thru-Z. Apply all these book's bonuses and tips to the areas need for your ghost kitchen start-up success. The chapters are written in a chronological order for you to go back if you need to troubleshoot and use as a study guide, to take your time and review. Use the business and marketing plan to fit your virtual menu after you decide on what to cook and serve out of your ghost kitchen delivery service.

God bless you all for taking the time out to read and achieve your goals or learn how to further your life dreams. I still have a whole bunch of NYC family who dream of opening up a restaurant to franchise all over. It's never too late. And for all those reading this book just for the money, and food isn't your passion market, at least learn the skill first, so you can know the whole business in-and-outs, versus looking from the outside in. It is better from experience to work in the business, and then on the business. Especially if you want to make max profit margins. It will also help you know where to problem-solve at, if the numbers in your kitchen are down regularly.

Any questions or comments, contact me via email: HitachiChoparazziAuthor@gmail.com. Leave reviews online on Amazon, Barnes & Noble, or anywhere books available. Please and thank you all! Blessings.

About Author

Hitachi Choparazzi is a New York City native, by way of Omaha, NE, who currently resides in Phoenix, AZ. Tattoo artist, shop owner, entrepreneur, turnt author.

He was the first Afro-American tattoo shop owner in Arizona. Ran the Chop Chop Tattoo Shop and Chop-A-Style Body Piercing 2-in-1 shop for years. Has over 17 years of tattoo experience. Learn how to tattoo from the inside being incarcerated for years and picking up a skillset with a passion and drive to be the best and deliver quality and consistency.

Hitachi Choparazzi started his own Chop-A-Style Publishing LLC company to help people incarcerated learn skillsets, personal development for their transition to help integrate back successfully into society. Also for entertainment with novels. Also his own library writing over 26 self-development and business development books and over 46 books and counting total. All from the inside.

Founder of Billion Dollar Blueprint movement and brand. Co-Founder of Incarcerated Lives Matter movement. Also Urban Bugatti shoes.

"This book is for y'all. I love to be of service, mentor, and educate y'all assist with skills and self-development. Love!"

Hitachichoparazziauthor@gmail.com
IG: Incarceratedauthor

Other Books and Scripts by the Author

Non-Fiction

- How to Rap; The Elementary Teaching of Hip-Hop

- How To Tattoo & Start-Up Business

- How To Digital Detox

- How To Start-Up a Food Truck Business

- How To Stop School and Mass Shootings: Dear Parents

- Incarcerated Lives Matter: The Hitachi Choparazzi Blueprint

- How to Love

- The Switch: A Social Awareness Self-Help

- Nipsey Hussle Lockdown Society Dedication–Tribute

- If Trayvon Martin Could Talk; Injustice

- How to do a Ghost Kitchen delivery service

Fiction

- The Eagle and Weasel (1-5 series kids' book)

- She Go! (urban novel)

- Reality Show 3D-HD (urban novel)

- Hot Thots (urban novel)

- Hot Thots 2

- Liqz (urban novel)

- Paranormal Whisper (horror novel)

- Pimp of Da Ratchets (urban novel)

- Pimp of Da Ratchets II Vegas (urban novel)

- Pimp of Da Ratchets 3 Orange is Da New Pimp (urban novel)

- Hitachi (urban novel)

- Penitentiary Pimp (urban novel)

- Weasel Society (urban novel)

- The Big Pep and Plucker Story-She Go! Prequel (urban novel)

Screenplays/Scripts

- Top Notch

- Hot Thots

- Pimp of Da Ratchets

- Weasel Society

- Million Dollar Games–A Secret Society

- The Eagle and Weasel (animation)

This one-of-a-kind How to Start-Up a Food Truck Business gives you an actual food truck blueprint, from the dos and don'ts to creating your unique dish and menu, then having people taste test first also includes how to register your food truck, marketing, and branding. How to pick out the right food truck and kitchen that caters to your menu. Prepare you for inspections from Health Department and the state. Advertisement, franchising, and all regulations of operations A-thru-Z made easy and in simplified comprehension to all. Teaches how to discover your theme and building on it while catering to consumers' demands and needs. The growth of your food truck margins and providing the ultimate customer service experience. This is Food Truck 101 for start-ups and first truck owners, a must-read for education, structure, and tips and bonuses that help you save time, money, and from making mistakes to put you out of business before it's a successful start-up off the ground. Finally how to source your food and find a distributor to lower cost per dish to increase truck revenues. This is the ultimate food truck guidebook in chronological order to study and learn these easy steps, and effective methods to implement. Also adopt the same professional food truck policy and ethical practices. You can have your own food truck business and be the entrepreneur you always wanted to be.

This *How to Do Cryptocurrency and NFTs* book provides you with new-wave era information and technology to add value and save you time of extensive research, to merely simplify and educate.

This book shows you not only how, but the what, why, and history, including marketing tips and how to build your NFT communities. Also how to create your own NFTs.

Finally where to get your NFTs done with certain blockchains you can use if you can't afford gas and minting fees. With a whole lot more of bonus tips of howto's.

This book is highly recommended for beginnings in the cryptocurrency space. Also the first-timers to creating their own NFTs A-thru-Z. 4th revolution revolves around information technology.

Billion Dollar Blueprint is a movement we challenge and inspire you to find your individual blueprint. Our mantra is "We believe everyone has their own blueprint like everyone has their own thumbprint". With these three core principles

Education

Elevation

Innovation

Hitachi Choparazzi is the founder and CEO. Orders available to support incarcerated businesses.

Orders available at: billiondollarblueprintmerch.com